Crochet Bakemono [monsters!]

spreading the love of making

Crochet Bakemono [monsters!]

BY LAN-ANH BUI & JOSEPHINE WAN

GUILD OF MASTER
CRAFTSMAN PUBLICATIONS

First published 2011 by
Guild of Master Craftsman
Publications Ltd
Castle Place, 166 High Street,
Lewes, East Sussex BN7 1XU

Text © Lan-Anh Bui
and Josephine Wan, 2011
Copyright in the Work
© GMC Publications Ltd, 2011

ISBN 978-1-86108-847-5

Publisher: Jonathan Bailey **Production Manager**: Jim Bulley **Managing Editor**: Gerrie Purcell
Senior Project Editor: Wendy McAngus **Editor**: Judith Chamberlain-Webber **Copy Writer**: Beth Wicks
Managing Art Editor: Gilda Pacitti **Art Editor**: Rebecca Mothersole **Photographer**: Rebecca Mothersole
Charts and pattern checking: Gina Alton **Technique illustrations**: Peters & Zabransky **Japanese translations**: Wei Xue
Set in Foundry Sans **Colour origination** by GMC Reprographics **Printed and bound** in China by 1010 Printing Ltd.

contents 🌸

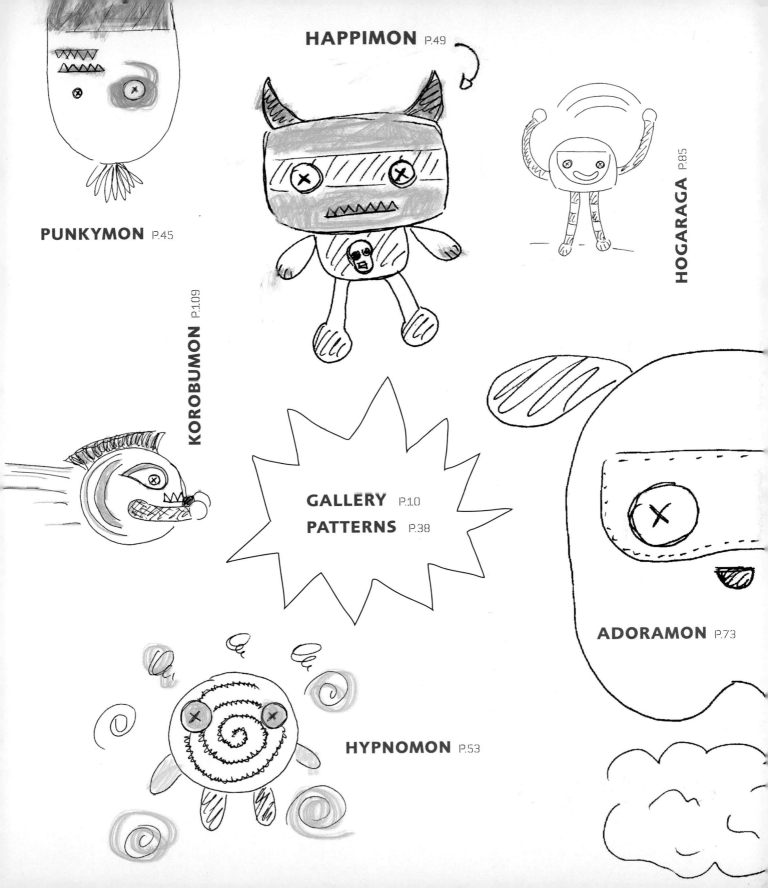

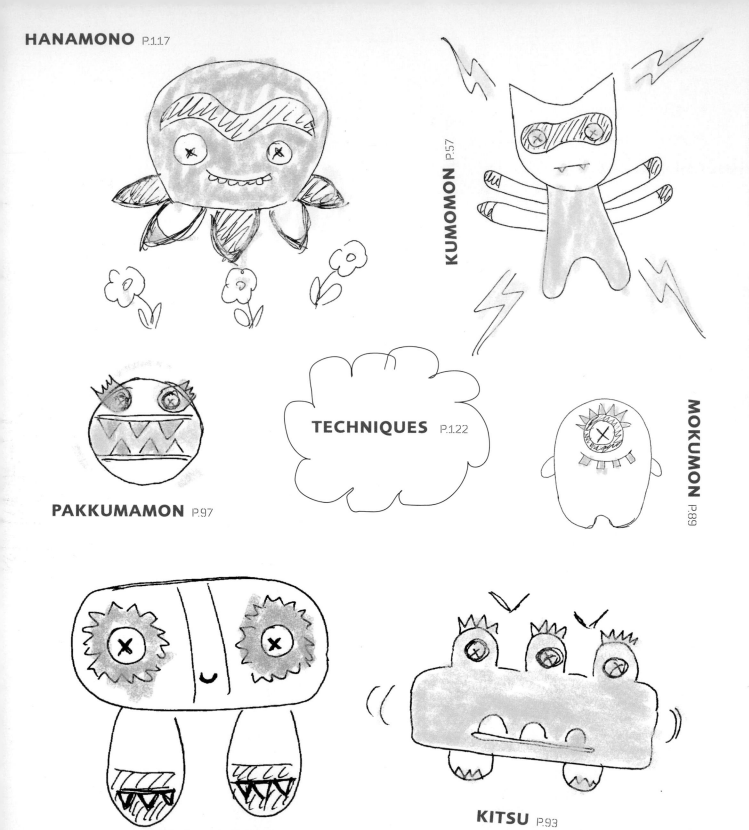

HANAMONO P.117

KUMOMON P.57

PAKKUMAMON P.97

TECHNIQUES P.122

MOKUMON P.89

JINKOU P.69

KITSU P.93

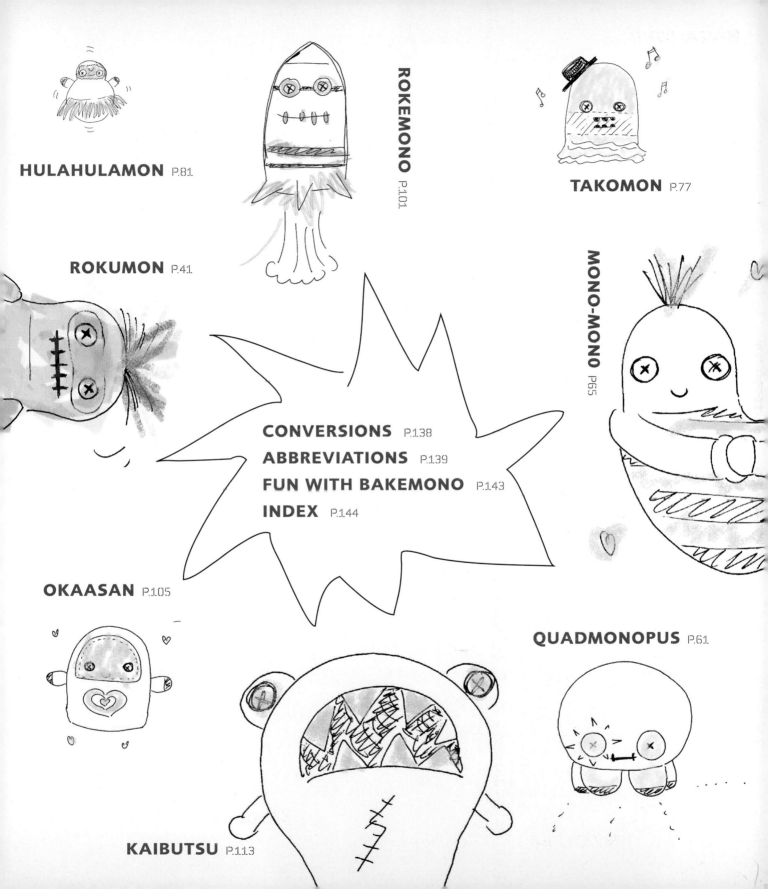

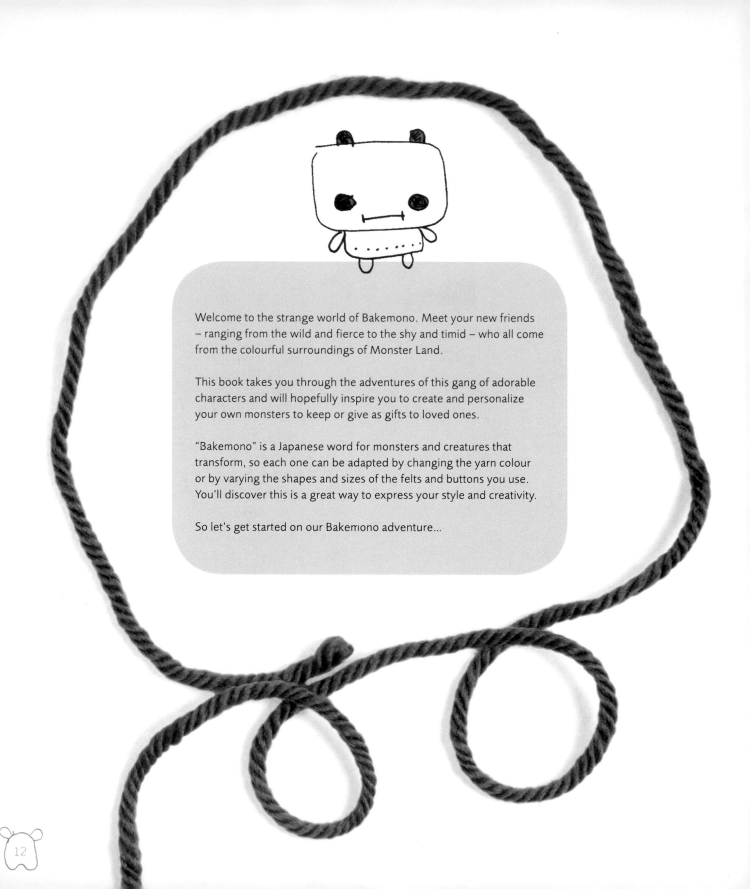

Welcome to the strange world of Bakemono. Meet your new friends – ranging from the wild and fierce to the shy and timid – who all come from the colourful surroundings of Monster Land.

This book takes you through the adventures of this gang of adorable characters and will hopefully inspire you to create and personalize your own monsters to keep or give as gifts to loved ones.

"Bakemono" is a Japanese word for monsters and creatures that transform, so each one can be adapted by changing the yarn colour or by varying the shapes and sizes of the felts and buttons you use. You'll discover this is a great way to express your style and creativity.

So let's get started on our Bakemono adventure...

bakemono are japanese creatures from another world who have the power to transform themselves into monsters. this one has evolved to become much more naughty over time.

ロクモン

ROKUMON
PATTERN ON PAGE 41

He refuses to have his hair cut and has dyed it all the colours of the rainbow; today it's **mellow yellow**.

Rokumon is an expert backgammon player and a fervent **eco warrior**.

Rokumon is always getting told off for **day dreaming** at school and for not speaking up in class, especially in **monster slang** classes.

Happily bungling along, teenager Rokumon is **still not sure what to make of life**. This week he's going to become a chef, last week his ambition was to be a famous drummer.

He can't stay still and is always dancing and singing along to his favourite Elvis songs.

He's as deaf as a doorpost and talks at maximum volume with a fake **Texas drawl**.

Destined to **make it big one day**, Punkymon is a loud and dynamic rockstar.

パンキモン

Punkymon never gets up before lunchtime and then only if his favourite meal of **cornflakes** and **olives** with **ice cream** is on offer.

His signature **red shorts** (which started off as green!) and **spiky hair** ensure that he stands out in a crowd.

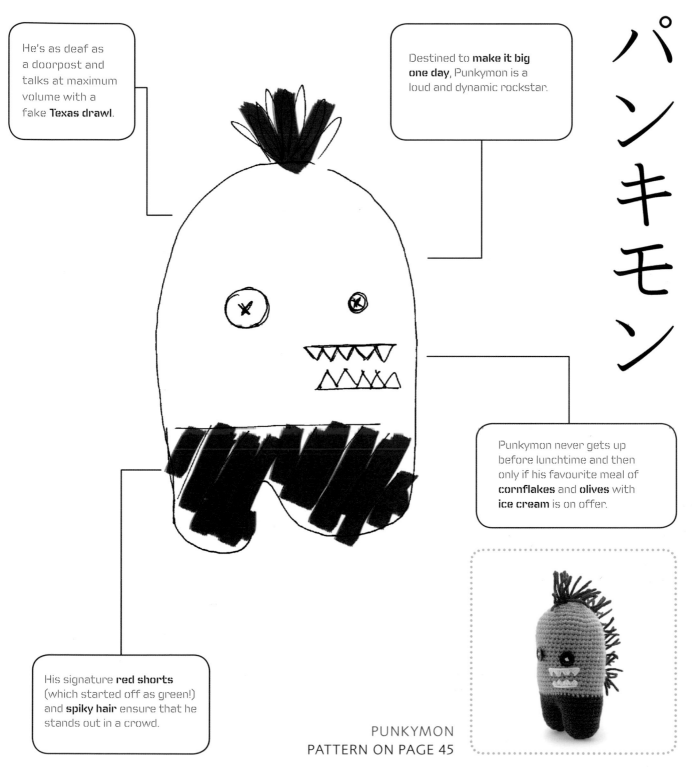

PUNKYMON
PATTERN ON PAGE 45

17

HAPPIMON
PATTERN
ON PAGE 49

幸せモン

Naughty, but nice, Happimon is a **loveable character** who is always getting up to mischief with his best friend **Mokumon**.

Together they **speed along on their skateboards**, seeking out opportunities for playing practical jokes on the other monsters or searching for exciting places to explore.

Happimon loves Mandarin oranges and **racing paper aeroplanes**.

He is well known for **popping up** in the most unexpected places.

催眠モン

Hypnomon set her heart on being a **trapeze artist,** but kept making herself **dizzy** and falling off the high platform.

All in a whirl, Hypnomon is an expert at **spinning a tale** and always attracts crowds of young monsters eager to hear the next **swashbuckling adventure** or **fairytale** fantasy.

Her peripheral vision makes her an ideal photographer for the fast-paced **Monster Paintball** Championships.

When the other monsters are not looking, Hypnomon loves jumping in puddles and **singing** in the rain at the top of her voice.

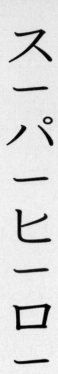
スーパーヒーロー

Is it a bird, is it a plane? No, it's Kumomon to the rescue. Superhero monster Kumomon is **lightning fast** and always the first one on the scene in a crisis, but with a knack of **causing havoc** rather than actually helping.

He **plays the clarinet** and likes pork and pink marmalade sausages.

When he's not saving Monster Land, Kumomon combines his acrobatic talents and **painting skills** to create colourful artistic masterpieces while playing the **steel drums**.

KUMOMON
PATTERN ON PAGE 57

臆病モン

Quadmonopus drinks endless quantities of strong tea with six sugars in each mug – perfect for dunking monster crackers in.

QUADMONOPUS
PATTERN ON PAGE 61

She also designs **her own range of stationery** for left-footed monsters and is a world-class hula hooper.

Quadmonopus is as timid and shy as they come. She is **multilingual** and can speak fluent Polish, Portuguese and Polynesian, but she speaks so quietly that no one can ever hear what she says.

21

モノモノ

**MONO-MONO
PATTERN ON PAGE 65**

Double trouble,
these two naughty
monsters never
agree on anything.

Being joined at the hip
does have its benefits
– Mono-mono are
the state **ping-pong
champions** and they
held an undefeated
record for badminton
doubles… until they
were disqualified for
throwing **marshmallows**
at each other.

Mono enjoys listening
to **Mozart**'s piano
concertos…

…his brother is a heavy
metal fan.

They both enjoy
cream teas, but the
brothers always end
up **fighting** over
whether the cream
or the jam should
go on first.

Jinkou is **a typical girl** and loves to shop until she drops, always coming home with bags of **novelty tea cozies** and collectible spoons.

JINKOU
PATTERN ON PAGE 69

ジンコ子

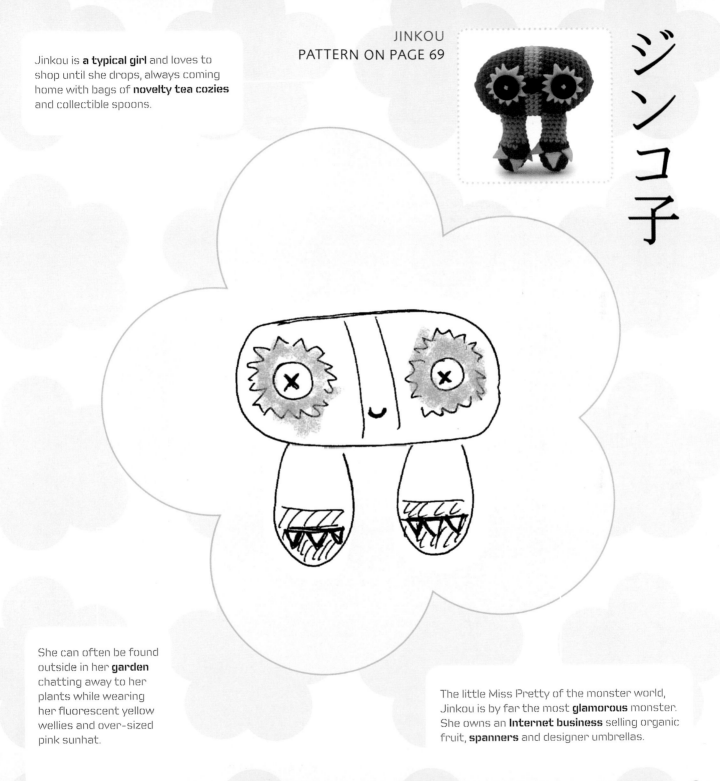

She can often be found outside in her **garden** chatting away to her plants while wearing her fluorescent yellow wellies and over-sized pink sunhat.

The little Miss Pretty of the monster world, Jinkou is by far the most **glamorous** monster. She owns an **Internet business** selling organic fruit, **spanners** and designer umbrellas.

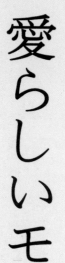
愛らしいモン

ADORAMON
PATTERN ON PAGE 73

With her **large flappy ears**, Adoramon listens in to conversations going on several miles away. She is an awful gossip, using her **keen sense of hearing** to discover exciting nuggets of information. She always wants to know what's going on and where the next party will be.

When she grows up Adoramon is going to be a movie star with **her own trailer** and her name up in lights. She has written long letters to her idols **Johnny Depp** and **Brad Pitt**, but they have yet to get back to her with an offer of a part.

タコモン

Takomon never goes out for tea without her **fancy black hat**. She is often accused of being a **perfectionist** and will polish her hat at least three times a day.

She is incredibly **ticklish** and, embarrassingly for her, occasionally **snorts** when she laughs.

Takomon has a **very sweet tooth** and can always be found chomping monster sugar canes and mint wasps.

She knows all the words to the Broadway showstoppers, but finds it impossible to **hold a tune** and torments the other monsters with her caterwauling.

TAKOMON
PATTERN ON PAGE 77

フラダンスモン

Hulahulamon always has to have everything in alphabetical order and has an impressive **photographic memory**.

Disco diva Hulahulamon likes nothing better than dressing up and dancing the night away. During the day she teaches belly dancing and jive, and on Wednesdays **quantum physics**.

In the evenings she can always be found on the dancefloor in her **Hawaiian skirt**, the newest addition to her dressing-up box.

HULAHULAMON
PATTERN ON PAGE 81

Last month she was sporting a very dapper glow-in-the-dark trilby with **matching gloves**.

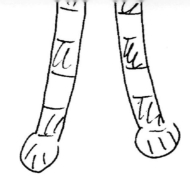

Hogaraga tried breakdancing classes, but they had to spend most of the lesson **unknotting** his legs. His party trick is spelling out **letters of the alphabet** with his legs, although he struggles with K.

ホガラカ

HOGARAGA
PATTERN ON PAGE 85

Whether rain or shine, he can always be seen out and about on his **unicycle**, turning left where he meant to go right and going down one-way streets in the **wrong direction**.

Hogaraga always mixes his words up and has a tendency to say them **back-to-front**.

He has difficulty with remembering directions and is **forever getting lost**.

27

ヒトモクモン

Mokumo's favourite party trick is **whistling** a four-note harmony through his teeth.

Mokumo's favourite party trick is **whistling** a four-note harmony through his teeth.

He is related to the famous **intrepid explorer** Nomukom, who discovered the island of the giant, hairless monsters.

MOKUMON
PATTERN ON PAGE 89

If there's any **trouble**, you can be certain Mokumon and his best mate Happimon have **something to do with it**.

He is addicted to **monster jelly beans** but spits out the green ones, because his mum once told him that they would turn his insides green.

Mokumo has a very **dry** sense of **humour** and is always amusing his teachers, who don't quite manage to **hide their smiles**.

With his **one large eye** Mokumo can seek out any leftover **sweets** from anywhere in the local neighbourhood.

木津

KITSU
PATTERN
ON PAGE 93

Three-eyed monster Kitsu spends the summer months at the monster swimming pools, teaching youngsters how to swim at the same time as **scanning the pool** for anyone in trouble.

In her youth, Kitsu was the **national synchronized swimming champion**, until they brought in the rule **banning snorkels**.

She loves **bubblegum** and can blow it into a wide range of amusing shapes, such as banana and sombrero. Kitsu also makes a **mean apple pie**, which she serves with lashings of thick, **lumpy** monster **gravy**.

パックマモン

Leave anything around, edible or not, and Pakkumamon will have consumed it in **just one bite**. He also has a tendency to talk continuously, often going off on long, extended tangents.

Pakkumamon is **not fussy**; he's happy talking to himself when no one else is around to listen. But be warned – get him on to the subject of **growing prize tomatoes** and you'll simply never hear the end of it.

Pakkumamon makes a living selling **chilli tomato cake** alongside platefuls of his signature dish of tomato, basil and banana jelly. He's also addicted to **sky diving**, but without a parachute. Pakkumamon simply **bounces along the ground** when he lands until eventually he comes to a stop, although this can take several days.

PAKKUMAMON
PATTERN ON PAGE 97

CROCHET BAKEMONO [monsters!]

ロクモン

Rokemono is always **blasting off** into another harebrained scheme, which inevitably leads to a crash landing back to reality. He aims high and gets **fantastic grades** at school, despite having his head in the clouds most of the time.

Rokemono is a **very intelligent** monster, but lacks **any common sense** whatsoever. He's always taking things apart to find out how they work, but unfortunately he has never quite got the hang of putting them back together afterwards.

Bursting with **energy**, Rokemono literally zooms around at **full speed**, crashing into anything and anyone coming the other way.

ROKEMONO
PATTERN ON PAGE 101

31

OKAASAN
PATTERN ON PAGE 105

お母さん

Okaasan has **irrational fears** of birds and dictionaries.

Okaasan is a **huggable** character radiating love and warmth. She's definitely the monster to have around when you're feeling down.

Okaasan can **chat** for hours and hours. Once she chatted to a friend in Australia on the phone for **five hours non-stop**, despite the fact that her friend had gone to bed two hours into the conversation.

Unfortunately, Okaasan is **incredibly clumsy** and is always tripping over shoes, burning the dinner and losing her glasses. You'd better take cover when she's playing monster **darts**.

KOROBUMON
PATTERN ON PAGE 109

転ぶモン

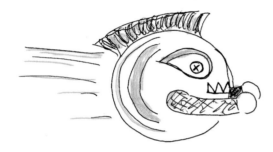

Korobumon's favourite pastime is driving at top speed in his cherry red **convertible** with go-faster stripes down the sides. Korobumon **dreams** about owning a **speedboat**, but he can't swim and he's scared of fish.

Korobumon is as **competitive** as they come, **overflowing with ambition**. Every year he enters the monster **cheese-rolling** competition and every year he's **disqualified** for hurling himself down the hill instead of the cheese.

He is banned from every **pub quiz** because Korobumon keeps grinding all the pencils down with his teeth, making an **ear-piercing** noise.

33

The young monsters all love Kaibutsu, especially when he makes his colourful balloon animals. They **fall about laughing** when he bites them and they burst in his face.

Kaibutsu hates his **tiny legs** and can often be found balanced precariously on top of his **wooden stilts**. He once tried to juggle while on the stilts, but he came crashing down, falling right into the monster pond.

KAIBUTSU
PATTERN ON PAGE 113

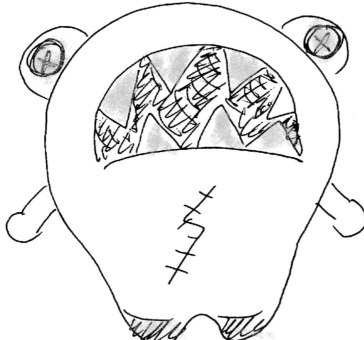

With his loud '**RAAAWWRRR**' and **sharp, pointed teeth**, Kaibutsu gives the impression that he's incredibly fierce and frightening, but in fact he's practising for the world's hottest-chilli-eating competition. Kaibutsu considers the **Scotch bonnet chilli** to be but a mere trifle.

As a **life-long hippy**, Hanamono firmly believes that everything can be **solved with a hug** or, if things are really dire, one of her **colourful cocktails**.

Hanamono is always dozing off, catching **40 winks** wherever she can, often mid-sentence or during job interviews, which could explain why she's never had a job.

Hanamono is **incredibly generous** and is always making things as gifts for other monsters.

Once, when pressing flowers for handmade cards, she managed to lose her **egg and cauliflower sandwich**, only to find it as **flat as a pancake** several days later.

HANAMONO
PATTERN ON PAGE 117

花モノ

A **fitness fanatic**, Hanamono fills her day with a strict regime of yoga, pilates and gentle jogging – nothing too strenuous.

35

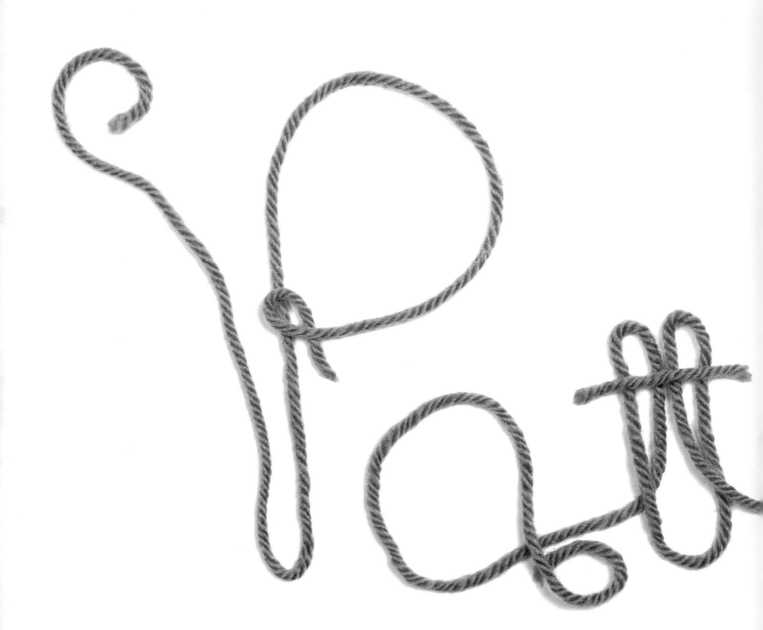

CROCHET BAKEMONO [monsters!]

YOU WILL NEED

- Debbie Bliss Cashmerino Aran 55% merino wool
  33% microfibre 12% cashmere (98yd/90m per 50g)
  25g green, 25g yellow, 25g pale blue

- 3.5mm (UK9:USE/4) crochet hook

- 2 black buttons (for eyes)

- Embroidery thread (black for mouth,
  white for sewing on button eyes)

- Polyester stuffing

Rokumon

Head

start with green

Round 1: Using magic circle technique – work 5 dc. (5 sts).
Round 2: 2dc into each st. (10 sts).
Round 3: (2dc in next dc, dc in next dc) to end. (15 sts).
Round 4: (2dc in next dc, dc in next 2 dc) to end. (20 sts).
Round 5: (2dc in next dc, dc in next 3 dc) to end. (25 sts).
Round 6: Dc to end. (25 sts).
Round 7: (2dc in next dc, dc in next 4 dc) to end. (30 sts).
Round 8: Dc to end. (30 sts).

introduce yellow

Round 9: Dc in next dc (10 x green), dc in next dc (10 x yellow), dc in next dc (10 x green). (30 sts).
Round 10: Dc in next dc (11 x green), dc in next dc (10 x yellow), dc in next dc (9 x green). (30 sts).
Round 11: Dc in next dc (12 x green), dc in next dc (10 x yellow), dc in next dc (8 x green). (30 sts).

work in green

Round 12: (2dc in next dc, dc in next 15 dc) to end. (32 sts).
Round 13: Dc to end. (32 sts).

Fasten off the work. Break off the yarn, leaving a tail for sewing.

Body

start with green

Round 1: Using magic circle technique – work 5 dc. (5 sts).
Round 2: 2dc into each st. (10 sts).
Round 3: (2dc in next dc, dc in next dc) to end. (15 sts).
Round 4: (2dc in next dc, dc in next 2 dc) to end. (20 sts).
Round 5: (2dc in next dc, dc in next 3 dc) to end. (25 sts).
Round 6: (2dc in next dc, dc in next 4 dc) to end. (30 sts).
Round 7: (2dc in next dc, dc in next 5 dc) to end. (35 sts).

change to blue

Round 8: (2dc in next dc, dc in next 6 dc) to end. (40 sts).
Round 9: Dc to end. (40 sts).

change to green

Round 10: (2dc in next dc, dc in next 9 dc) to end. (44 sts).

change to yellow

Round 11: Dc to end. (44 sts).
Round 12: (Dc in next 9 dc, dc2tog) to end. (40 sts).

change to blue

Round 13: (Dc in next 18 dc, dc2tog) to end. (38 sts).

change to green

Round 14: Dc to end. (38 sts).
Round 15: (Dc in next 17 dc, dc2tog) to end. (36 sts).

change to yellow

Round 16: (Dc in next 16 dc, dc2tog) to end. (34 sts).

change to blue

Round 17: Dc to end. (34 sts).
Round 18: (Dc in next 15 dc, dc2tog) to end. (32 sts).

change to green

Rounds 19–21: Dc to end. (32 sts).

Fasten off the work. Break off the yarn, leaving a tail for sewing.

Arms (make 2 alike)

start with yellow

Round 1: Using magic circle technique – work 5 dc. (5 sts).
Round 2: 2dc into each st. (10 sts).
Round 3: (2dc in next dc, dc in next 4 dc) to end. (12 sts).

change to green

Rounds 4–6: Dc to end. (12 sts).
Round 7: Dc2tog, then dc rem sts. (11 sts).
Round 8: Dc to end. (11 sts).
Round 9: Dc2tog, then dc rem sts. (10 sts).
Round 10: Dc to end. (10 sts).
Round 11: Dc2tog, then dc rem sts. (9 sts).
Round 12: Dc2tog, then dc rem sts. (8 sts).

Fasten off the work. Break off the yarn, leaving a tail for sewing.

Making up

With the white embroidery thread sew on the buttons for the eyes and embroider the mouth with the black. For the hair, thread strands of yellow yarn on to the head until you reach the desired thickness and then trim the ends to the desired length (see page 136). Stuff all the parts, then sew the head and arms to the body. Weave in any loose ends.

HEAD

Round	Stitches	Colour
1	MC5	Green
2	10 (inc 5)	Green
3	15 (inc 5)	Green
4	20 (inc 5)	Green
5	25 (inc 5)	Green
6	25	Green
7	30 (inc 5)	Green
8	30	Green
9–11	30	G, Y, G
12	32 (inc 2)	Green
13	32	Green

BODY

Round	Stitches	Colour
1	MC5	Green
2	10 (inc 5)	Green
3	15 (inc 5)	Green
4	20 (inc 5)	Green
5	25 (inc 5)	Green
6	30 (inc 5)	Green
7	35 (inc 5)	Green
8	40 (inc 5)	Blue
9	40	Blue
10	44 (inc 4)	Green
11	44	Yellow
12	40 (dec 4)	Yellow
13	38 (dec 2)	Blue
14	38	Green
15	36 (dec 2)	Green
16	34 (dec 2)	Yellow
17	34	Blue
18	32 (dec 2)	Blue
19–21	32	Green

ARMS

Round	Stitches	Colour
1	MC5	Yellow
2	10 (inc 5)	Yellow
3	12 (inc 2)	Yellow
4–6	12	Green
7	11 (dec 1)	Green
8	11	Green
9	10 (dec 1)	Green
10	10	Green
11	9 (dec 1)	Green
12	8 (dec 1)	Green

i am an anarchist

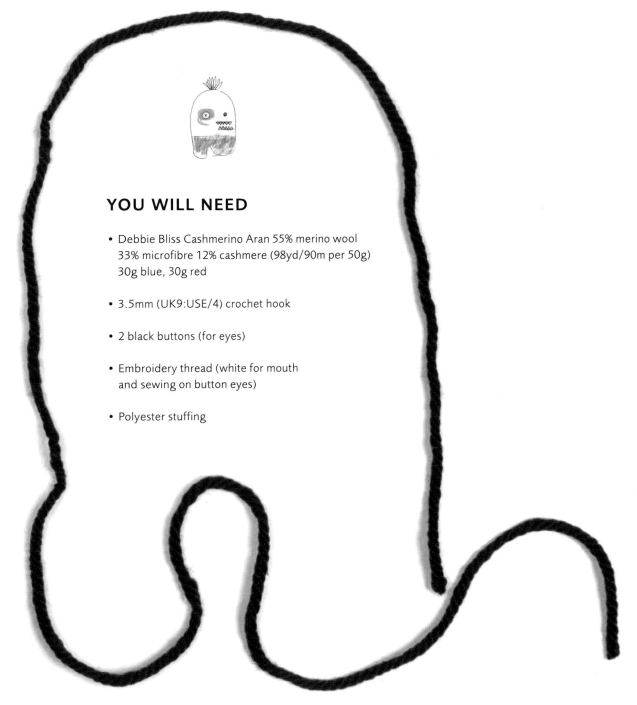

YOU WILL NEED

• Debbie Bliss Cashmerino Aran 55% merino wool
33% microfibre 12% cashmere (98yd/90m per 50g)
30g blue, 30g red

• 3.5mm (UK9:USE/4) crochet hook

• 2 black buttons (for eyes)

• Embroidery thread (white for mouth
and sewing on button eyes)

• Polyester stuffing

Punkymon

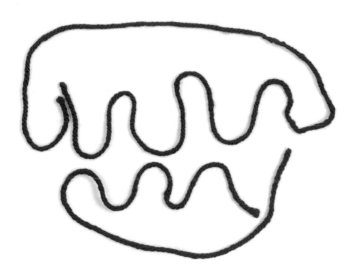

Body and legs

start with blue

Round 1: Using magic circle technique – work 6 dc. (6 sts).
Round 2: 2dc into each st. (12 sts).
Round 3: (2dc in next dc, dc in next dc) to end. (18 sts).
Round 4: (2dc in next dc, dc in next 2 dc) to end. (24 sts).
Round 5: (2dc in next dc, dc in next 3 dc) to end. (30 sts).
Round 6: (2dc in next dc, dc in next 4 dc) to end. (36 sts).
Round 7: (2dc in next dc, dc in next 5 dc) to end. (42 sts).
Round 8: (2dc in next dc, dc in next 6 dc) to end. (48 sts).
Rounds 9–25: Dc to end. (48 sts).

change to red

Rounds 26–30: Dc to end. (48 sts).
Sew on the buttons for the eyes with the white embroidery thread, and embroider the mouth as shown using running stitch. To form 2 legs (Leg A and Leg B), continue from body part.

Leg A

continue in red

Round 31a: Dc around 24 sts, then join into first stitch. (24 sts).
Round 32a–34a: Dc to end. (24 sts).
Round 35a: (Dc in next 4 dc, dc2tog) to end. (20 sts).
Round 36a: (Dc in next 3 dc, dc2tog) to end. (16 sts).
Round 37a: (Dc in next 2 dc, dc2tog) to end. (12 sts).
Round 38a: (Dc2tog) to end. (6 sts).
Fasten off the work. Break off the yarn, leaving a tail for sewing. Thread the end through rem sts, then pull tight and secure with a knot. Hide the tail of the yarn (see page 136). Stuff the body and leg A.

Leg B

continue in red

Round 31b: Dc around 24 sts, then join into first stitch. (24 sts).
Rounds 32b–34b: Dc to end. (24 sts).
Round 35b: (Dc in next 4 dc, dc2tog) to end. (20 sts).
Round 36b: (Dc in next 3 dc, dc2tog) to end. (16 sts).
Round 37b: (Dc in next 2 dc, dc2tog) to end. (12 sts).
Round 38b: (Dc2tog) to end. (6 sts).
Stuff leg B.
Fasten off the work. Break off the yarn, leaving a tail for sewing. Thread the end through rem sts, then pull tight and secure with a knot. Hide the tail of the yarn (see page 136).

Making up

Weave in any loose ends. Using the red yarn, loop and knot to form Mohican hair (see page 136).

generous teeth

BODY AND LEGS

Round	Stitches	Colour
1	MC6	Blue
2	12 (inc 6)	Blue
3	18 (inc 6)	Blue
4	24 (inc 6)	Blue
5	30 (inc 6)	Blue
6	36 (inc 6)	Blue
7	42 (inc 6)	Blue
8	48 (inc 6)	Blue
9–25	48	Blue
26–30	48	Red
Begin legs		
31a/b	24 – rejoin to first st	Red
32–34a/b	24	Red
35a/b	20 (dec 4)	Red
36a/b	16 (dec 4)	Red
37a/b	12 (dec 4)	Red
38a/b	6 (dec 6)	Red
Stuff and close		
Loop and knot yarn to form Mohican hair		

happiness is a state of mind

CROCHET BAKEMONO [monsters!]

YOU WILL NEED

- Debbie Bliss Cashmerino Aran 55% merino wool 33% microfibre 12% cashmere (98yd/90m per 50g) 25g light blue, 25g dark blue

- 3.5mm (UK9:USE/4) crochet hook

- 2 black buttons (for eyes)

- Small square of black felt (for skull logo)

- Embroidery thread (black for mouth, blue for talons, white for sewing on button eyes and skull detail)

- Polyester stuffing

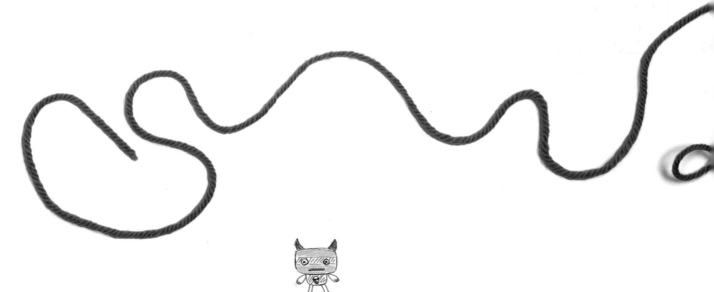

Happimon

Head
start with light blue
Round 1: Using magic circle technique – work 6 dc. (6 sts).
Round 2: 2dc into each st. (12 sts).
Round 3: (2dc in next dc, dc in next dc) to end. (18 sts).
Round 4: (2dc in next dc, dc in next 2 dc) to end. (24 sts).
Round 5: (2dc in next dc, dc in next 3 dc) to end. (30 sts).
Round 6: (2dc in next dc, dc in next 4 dc) to end. (36 sts).
Round 7: (2dc in next dc, dc in next 5 dc) to end. (42 sts).
Round 8: (2dc in next dc, dc in next 6 dc) to end. (48 sts).
Round 9: Into back loop: dc to end. (48 sts).
Rounds 10–14: Dc to end. (48 sts).
change to dark blue
Rounds 15–16: Dc to end. (48 sts).
change to light blue
Rounds 17–19: Dc to end. (48 sts).
Round 20: Into back loop: dc to end. (48 sts).
Round 21: (Dc in next 6dc, dc2tog) to end. (42 sts).
Sew on the eyes with the white embroidery thread and embroider the mouth with the black using darned lines as shown.
Round 22: (Dc in next 5 dc, dc2tog) to end. (36 sts).
Round 23: (Dc in next 4 dc, dc2tog) to end. (30 sts).
Round 24: (Dc in next 3 dc, dc2tog) to end. (24 sts).
Fasten off the work. Break off the yarn, leaving a tail for sewing then stuff the head.

Horns (make 2 alike)
use dark blue
Round 1: Using magic circle technique – work 4 dc. (4 sts).
Round 2: 2dc into each st. (8 sts).
Rounds 3–5: Dc to end. (8 sts).
Round 6: 2dc in next dc, dc remaining dc. (9 sts).
Round 7: Dc to end. (9 sts).
Fasten off the work. Break off the yarn, leaving a tail for sewing. Stuff the horns then sew them onto the head.

Body
use dark blue
Round 1: Using magic circle technique – work 6 dc. (6 sts).
Round 2: 2dc into each st. (12 sts).
Round 3: (2dc in next dc, dc in next dc) to end. (18 sts).
Round 4: (2dc in next dc, dc in next 2 dc) to end. (24 sts).
Rounds 5–10: Dc to end. (24 sts).
Cut a skull shape from felt and sew to the body with white embroidery thread. Stuff the body then sew the head to the body.

Legs (make 2 alike)
start with dark blue
Round 1: Using magic circle technique – work 5 dc. (5 sts).
Round 2: 2dc into each st. (10 sts).
Round 3: (2dc in next dc, dc in next dc) to end. (15 sts).
Round 4: (2dc in next dc, dc in next 2 dc) to end. (20 sts).
Rounds 5–6: Dc to end. (20 sts).
Round 7: (Dc in next 2dc, dc2tog) to end. (15 sts).
Round 8: (Dc in next dc, dc2tog) to end. (10 sts).
Partially stuff the legs.
change to light blue
Rounds 9–13: Dc to end. (10 sts).
Fasten off the work. Break off the yarn leaving a tail for sewing. Finish stuffing the legs then attach them to the body.

Arms (make 2 alike)
use light blue
Round 1: Using magic circle technique – work 5 dc. (5 sts).
Round 2: 2dc into each st. (10 sts).
Rounds 3–5: Dc to end. (10 sts).
Round 6: Dc2tog, dc around rem sts. (9 sts).
Round 7: Dc2tog, dc around rem sts. (8 sts).
Round 8: Dc2tog, dc around rem sts. (7 sts).
Round 9: Dc2tog, dc around rem sts. (6 sts).
Fasten off the work.
Break off yarn leaving a tail for sewing.
Stuff the arms then attach them to the body.

Making up
Embroider the talons with blue embroidery thread using darned lines as shown. Weave in any loose ends.

HEAD

Round	Stitches	Colour
1	MC6	Light blue
2	12 (inc 6)	Light blue
3	18 (inc 6)	Light blue
4	24 (inc 6)	Light blue
5	30 (inc 6)	Light blue
6	36 (inc 6)	Light blue
7	42 (inc 6)	Light blue
8	48 (inc 6)	Light blue
9	Into back loops 48	Light blue
10–14	48	Light blue
15–16	48	Dark blue
17–19	48	Light blue
20	Into back loops 48	Light blue
21	42 (dec 6)	Light blue
Sew on eyes, embroider mouth		
22	36 (dec 6)	Light blue
23	30 (dec 6)	Light blue
24	24 (dec 6)	Light blue

HORNS

Round	Stitches	Colour
1	MC 4	Dark blue
2	8 (inc 4)	Dark blue
3–5	8	Dark blue
6	9 (inc 1)	Dark blue
7	9	Dark blue

BODY

Round	Stitches	Colour
1	MC 6	Dark blue
2	12 (inc 6)	Dark blue
3	18 (inc 6)	Dark blue
4	24 (inc 6)	Dark blue
5–10	24	Dark blue

LEGS

Round	Stitches	Colour
1	MC 5	Dark blue
2	10 (inc 5)	Dark blue
3	15 (inc 5)	Dark blue
4	20 (inc 5)	Dark blue
5–6	20	Dark blue
7	15 (dec 5)	Dark blue
8	10 (dec 5)	Dark blue
Partially stuff		
9–13	10	Light blue

ARMS

Round	Stitches	Colour
1	MC 5	Light blue
2	10 (inc 5)	Light blue
3–5	10	Light blue
6	9 (dec 1)	Light blue
7	8 (dec 1)	Light blue
8	7 (dec 1)	Light blue
9	6 (dec 1)	Light blue

you will be hypnotized

you will be hypnotized

you will be hypnotized

CROCHET BAKEMONO [monsters!]

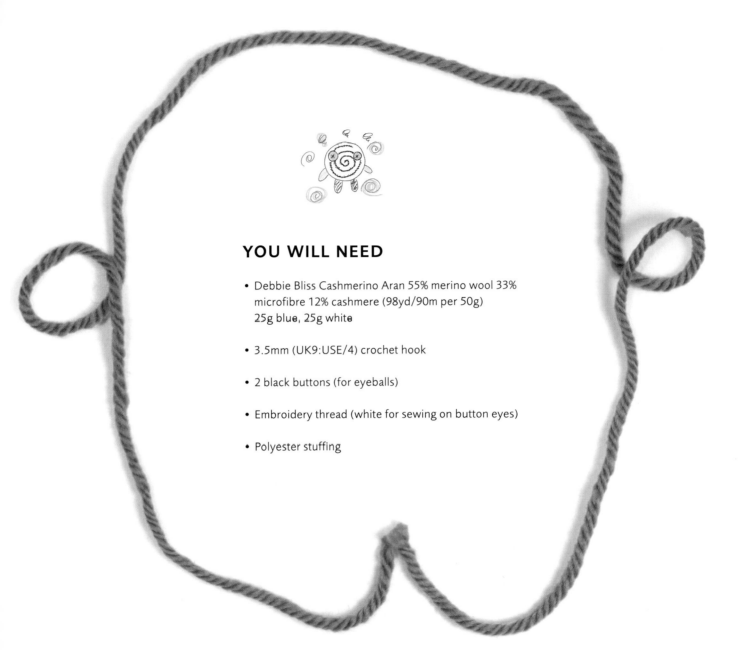

YOU WILL NEED

- Debbie Bliss Cashmerino Aran 55% merino wool 33% microfibre 12% cashmere (98yd/90m per 50g) 25g blue, 25g white

- 3.5mm (UK9:USE/4) crochet hook

- 2 black buttons (for eyeballs)

- Embroidery thread (white for sewing on button eyes)

- Polyester stuffing

Hypnomon

53

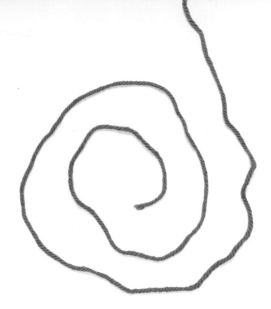

Eye backings (make 2 alike)

use blue

Round 1: Using magic circle technique – work 6 dc. (6 sts).
Round 2: 2dc into each st. (12 sts).
Rounds 3–4: Dc to end. (12 sts).
Fasten off the work. Break off the yarn, leaving a tail for sewing.
Sew on the buttons for eyeballs.
Lightly stuff the eye backings.

Head

start with white (alternate 2 rounds white
with 1 round blue)

Round 1: Using magic circle technique – work 6 dc. (6 sts).
Round 2: 2dc into each st (12 sts).
Round 3: (2dc in next dc, dc in next dc) to end. (18 sts).
Round 4: (2dc in next dc, dc in next 2 dc) to end. (24 sts).
Round 5: (2dc in next dc, dc in next 3 dc) to end. (30 sts).
Round 6: (2dc in next dc, dc in next 4 dc) to end. (36 sts).
Round 7: (2dc in next dc, dc in next 5 dc) to end. (42 sts).
Round 8: (2dc in next dc, dc in next 6 dc) to end. (48 sts).
Rounds 9–12: Dc to end. (48 sts).
Round 13: (Dc in next 6 dc, dc2tog) to end. (42 sts).
Round 14: (Dc in next 5 dc, dc2tog) to end. (36 sts).
Round 15: (Dc in next 4 dc, dc2tog) to end. (30 sts).
Round 16: (Dc in next 3 dc, dc2tog) to end. (24 sts).
Stuff the head.

Round 17: (Dc in next 2 dc, dc2tog) to end. (18 sts).
Round 18: (Dc in next dc, dc2tog) to end. (12 sts).
Round 19: (Dc2tog) to end. (6 sts).
Round 20: (Dc2tog) to end. (3 sts).
Fasten off the work. Break off the yarn, leaving a tail for sewing.
Thread the end through rem sts, then pull tight and secure with
a knot. Hide the tail of the yarn (see page 136). Sew the eyes
onto the head.

Legs (make 2 alike)

use blue

Round 1: Using magic circle technique – work 5 dc. (5 sts).
Round 2: 2dc into each st. (10 sts).
Rounds 3–10: Dc to end. (10 sts).
Fasten off the work. Break off the yarn, leaving a tail for sewing.
Stuff the legs then sew them to the body.

Arms (make 2 alike)

start with blue

Round 1: Using magic circle technique – work 4 dc. (4 sts).
Round 2: 2 dc into each st. (8 sts).
Round 3: Dc to end. (8 sts).
change to white
Rounds 4–8: Dc to end. (8 sts).
Fasten off the work. Break off the yarn, leaving a tail for sewing.
Stuff the arms then sew them to the body.

Making up

Weave in any loose ends.

EYE BACKINGS

Round	Stitches	Colour
1	MC6	Blue
2	12 (inc 6)	Blue
3–4	12	Blue

LEGS

Round	Stitches	Colour
1	MC 5	Blue
2	10 (inc 5)	Blue
3–10	10	Blue

ARMS

Round	Stitches	Colour
1	MC 4	Blue
2	8 (inc 4)	Blue
3	8	Blue
4–8	8	White

HEAD

Round	Stitches	Colour
1	MC 6	White
2	12 (inc 6)	White
3	18 (inc 6)	Blue
4	24 (inc 6)	White
5	30 (inc 6)	White
6	36 (inc 6)	Blue
7	42 (inc 6)	White
8	48 (inc 6)	White
9	48	Blue
10	48	White
11	48	White
12	48	Blue
13	42 (dec 6)	White
14	36 (dec 6)	White
15	30 (dec 6)	Blue
16	24 (dec 6)	White
Stuff		
17	18 (dec 6)	White
18	12 (dec 6)	Blue
19	6 (dec 6)	White
20	3 (dec 3)	White

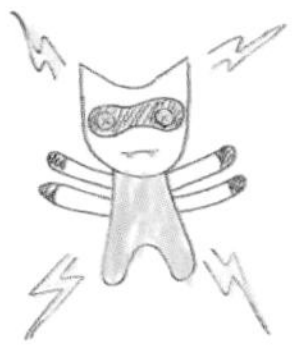

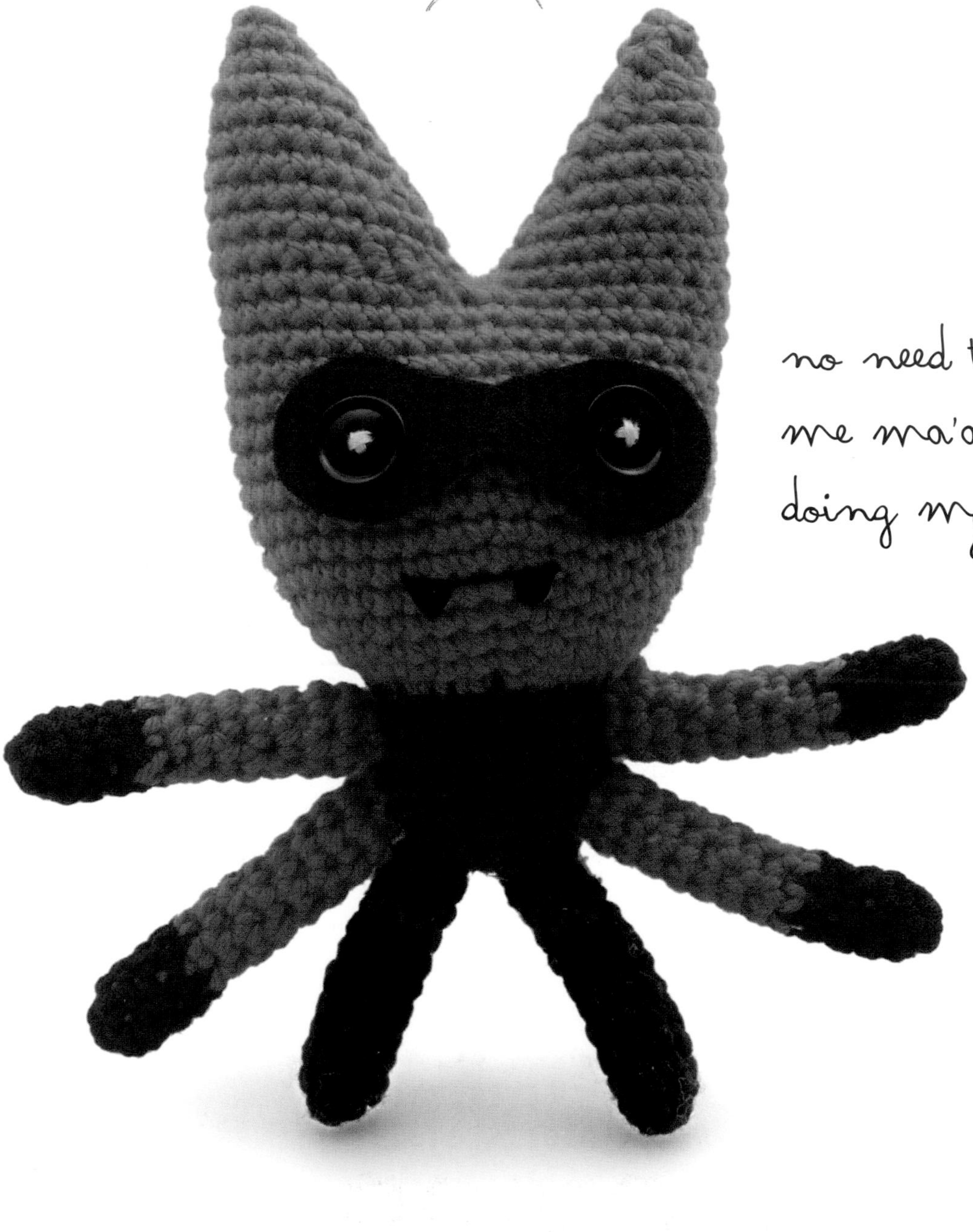

no need to thank me ma'am, i'm just doing my job

YOU WILL NEED

- Debbie Bliss Cashmerino Aran 55% merino wool 33% microfibre 12% cashmere (98yd/90m per 50g)
  25g yellow, 15g red, 10g black

- 3.5mm (UK9:USE/4) crochet hook

- 2 black buttons (for eyes)

- Small piece of red felt (for eyepiece)

- Embroidery thread (black for mouth, white for sewing on button eyes)

- Polyester stuffing

Kumomon

Head and ears
use yellow

Round 1: Using magic circle technique – work 5 dc. (5 sts).
Round 2: 2dc into each st. (10 sts).
Round 3: (2dc in next dc, dc in next dc) to end. (15 sts).
Round 4: (2dc in next dc, dc in next 2 dc) to end. (20 sts).
Round 5: (2dc in next dc, dc in next 3 dc) to end. (25 sts).
Round 6: (2dc in next dc, dc in next 4 dc) to end. (30 sts).
Round 7: (2dc in next dc, dc in next 5 dc) to end. (35 sts).
Round 8: (2dc in next dc, dc in next 6 dc) to end. (40 sts).
Rounds 9–18: Dc to end. (40 sts).

Ear A
continue in yellow

Round 19a: Dc around 20 sts, then join into first stitch. (20 sts).
Round 20a: Dc to end. (20 sts).
Sew on the felt eyepiece using embroidery stitch or running stitch (or use fabric glue). Sew on the buttons for the eyes with white embroidery thread.
Embroider the mouth using running stitch with black embroidery thread. Partially stuff the head.
Round 21a: Dc2tog, dc to last 2 sts, dc2tog. (18 sts).
Round 22a: Dc2tog, dc to last 2 sts, dc2tog. (16 sts).
Round 23a: Dc2tog, dc to last 2 sts, dc2tog. (14 sts).
Round 24a: Dc2tog, dc to last 2 sts, dc2tog. (12 sts).
Round 25a: Dc2tog, dc to last 2 sts, dc2tog. (10 sts).
Stuff the head and ears tightly.
Round 26a: Dc2tog, dc to last 2 sts, dc2tog. (8 sts).
Round 27a: Dc2tog, dc to last 2 sts, dc2tog. (6 sts).
Round 28a: Dc2tog, dc to last 2 sts, dc2tog. (4 sts).
Fasten off the work. Break off the yarn, leaving a tail for sewing. Thread the end through rem sts, then pull tight and secure with a knot. Hide the tail of the yarn (see page 136).

Ear B
continue in yellow

Rejoin the yarn to the middle of the top of the head.
Round 19b: Dc around 20 rem sts of round 18, then join into first stitch. (20 sts).
Round 20b: Dc to end. (20 sts).
Rounds 21b–28b: Work as for rounds 21a–28a and finish off as for ear A.

Body
use red

Round 1: Using magic circle technique – work 5 dc. (5 sts).
Round 2: 2dc into each st. (10 sts).
Round 3: (2dc in next dc, dc in next dc) to end. (15 sts).
Round 4: (2dc in next dc, dc in next 2 dc) to end. (20 sts).
Rounds 5–8: Dc to end. (20 sts).
Fasten off the work. Break off the yarn, leaving a tail for sewing. Stuff the body then sew it to the head.

Legs (make 2 alike)
start with black

Round 1: Using magic circle technique – work 6 dc. (6 sts).
Rounds 2–8: Dc to end. (6 sts).
change to red
Rounds 9–11: Dc to end. (6 sts).
Fasten off the work. Break off the yarn, leaving a tail for sewing. Stuff the legs then sew them to the body.

Arms (make 4 alike)
start with red

Round 1: Using magic circle technique – work 6 dc. (6 sts).
Rounds 2–5: Dc to end. (6 sts).
change to yellow
Rounds 6–13: Dc to end. (6 sts).
Fasten off the work. Break off the yarn, leaving a tail for sewing. Stuff the arms then sew them to the body.

Making up
Weave in any loose ends.

HEAD

Round	Stitches	Colour
1	MC5	Yellow
2	10 (inc 5)	Yellow
3	15 (inc 5)	Yellow
4	20 (inc 5)	Yellow
5	25 (inc 5)	Yellow
6	30 (inc 5)	Yellow
7	35 (inc 5)	Yellow
8	40 (inc 5)	Yellow
9–18	40	Yellow
Divide for ears		
19a/b–20a/b	20	Yellow
21a/b	18 (dec 2)	Yellow
22a/b	16 (dec 2)	Yellow
23a/b	14 (dec 2)	Yellow
24a/b	12 (dec 2)	Yellow
25a/b	10 (dec 2)	Yellow
Stuff tightly		
26a/b	8 (dec 2)	Yellow
27a/b	6 (dec 2)	Yellow
28a/b	4 (dec 2)	Yellow

BODY

Round	Stitches	Colour
1	MC5	Red
2	10 (inc 5)	Red
3	15 (inc 5)	Red
4	20 (inc 5)	Red
5–8	20	Red

LEGS

Round	Stitches	Colour
1	MC6	Black
2–8	6	Black
9–11	6	Red

ARMS

Round	Stitches	Colour
1	MC6	Red
2–5	6	Red
6–13	6	Yellow

two legs good, four legs better

CROCHET BAKEMONO [monsters!]

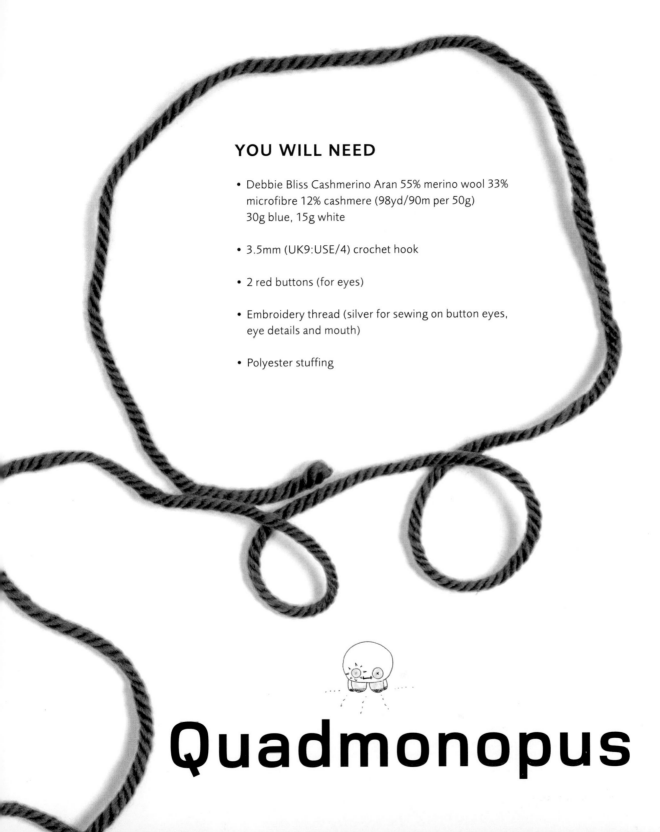

YOU WILL NEED

- Debbie Bliss Cashmerino Aran 55% merino wool 33% microfibre 12% cashmere (98yd/90m per 50g) 30g blue, 15g white

- 3.5mm (UK9:USE/4) crochet hook

- 2 red buttons (for eyes)

- Embroidery thread (silver for sewing on button eyes, eye details and mouth)

- Polyester stuffing

Quadmonopus

oh my starry-eyed monster

Head
use blue
Round 1: Using magic circle technique – work 6 dc. (6 sts).
Round 2: 2dc into each st. (12 sts).
Round 3: (2dc in next dc, dc in next dc) to end. (18 sts).
Round 4: (2dc in next dc, dc in next 2 dc) to end. (24 sts).
Round 5: (2dc in next dc, dc in next 3 dc) to end. (30 sts).
Round 6: (2dc in next dc, dc in next 4 dc) to end. (36 sts).
Round 7: (2dc in next dc, dc in next 5 dc) to end. (42 sts).
Row 8: (2dc in next dc, dc in next 6 dc) to end. (48 sts).
Rounds 9–16: Dc to end (48 sts).
Row 17: (dc in next 6 dc, dc2tog) to end. (42 sts).
Sew on the eyes and embroider the eye details and mouth using running stitch with silver embroidery thread.
Round 18: (Dc in next 5 dc, dc2tog) to end. (36 sts).
Round 19: (Dc in next 4 dc, dc2tog) to end. (30 sts).
Round 20: (Dc in next 3 dc, dc2tog) to end. (24 sts).
Stuff the head firmly.
Round 21: (Dc in next 2 dc, dc2tog) to end. (18 sts).
Round 22: (Dc in next dc, dc2tog) to end. (12 sts).
Round 23: (Dc2tog) to end. (6 sts).
Fasten off the work. Break off the yarn, leaving a tail for sewing. Thread the end through rem sts, then pull tight and secure with a knot. Hide the tail of the yarn (see page 136).

Legs (make 4 alike)
start with blue
Round 1: Using magic circle technique – work 5 dc. (5 sts).
Round 2: 2dc into each st. (10 sts).
Round 3: (2dc in next dc, dc in next 4 dc) to end. (12 sts).
Round 4: Dc to end. (12 sts).
change to white
Rounds 5–7: Dc to end. (12 sts).
Fasten off the work. Break off the yarn, leaving a tail for sewing. Stuff the legs then sew them to the body.

Making up
Weave in any loose ends.

HEAD

Round	Stitches	Colour
1	MC 6	Blue
2	12 (inc 6)	Blue
3	18 (inc 6)	Blue
4	24 (inc 6)	Blue
5	30 (inc 6)	Blue
6	36 (inc 6)	Blue
7	42 (inc 6)	Blue
8	48	Blue
9–16	48	Blue
17	42 (dec 6)	Blue
Sew on eyes and mouth		
18	36 (dec 6)	Blue
19	30 (dec 6)	Blue
20	24 (dec 6)	Blue
Stuff		
21	18 (dec 6)	Blue
22	12 (dec 6)	Blue
23	6 (dec 6)	Blue

LEGS

Round	Stitches	Colour
1	MC 5	Blue
2	10 (inc 5)	Blue
3	12 (inc 2)	Blue
4	12	Blue
5–7	12	White

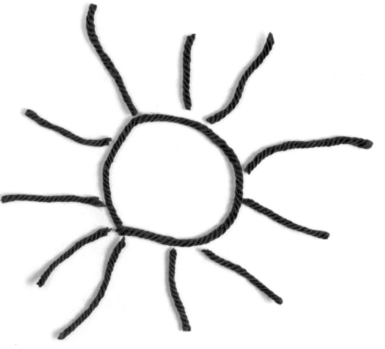

we agree to disagree

 CROCHET BAKEMONO [monsters!]

YOU WILL NEED

- Debbie Bliss Cashmerino Aran 55% merino wool 33% microfibre 12% cashmere (98yd/90m per 50g) 50g red, 50g black, 10g blue, 10g pink

- 3.5mm (UK9:USE/4) crochet hook

- 4 black buttons (for eyes)

- Embroidery thread (pink and blue for mouths and sewing on button eyes)

- Polyester stuffing

Mono-mono

Body and heads

start with black (alternate 2 rows black with 2 rows red)

Round 1: Using magic circle technique – work 7 dc. (7 sts).
Round 2: 2dc into each st. (14 sts).
Round 3: (2dc in next dc, dc in next dc) to end. (21 sts).
Round 4: (2dc in next dc, dc in next 2 dc) to end. (28 sts).
Round 5: (2dc in next dc, dc in next 3 dc) to end. (35 sts).
Round 6: (2dc in next dc, dc in next 4 dc) to end. (42 sts).
Round 7: (2dc in next dc, dc in next 5 dc) to end. (49 sts).
Round 8: (2dc in next dc, dc in next 6 dc) to end. (56 sts).
Rounds 9–20: Dc to end. (56 sts).
Partially stuff.

Head A

change to pink for head A

Round 21a: Dc around 28 sts, then join into first stitch. (28 sts).
Rounds 22a–27a: Dc to end. (28 sts).
Embroider the mouth as shown with pink and blue embroidery thread.
Round 28a: (Dc in next 5 dc, dc2tog) to end. (24 sts).
Round 29a: (Dc in next 4 dc, dc2tog) to end. (20 sts).
Round 30a: (Dc in next 3 dc, dc2tog) to end. (16 sts).
Sew two buttons onto the head for the eyes with pink and blue embroidery thread to match the colour of the head. Stuff the head firmly.
Round 31a: (Dc in next 2 dc, dc2tog) to end. (12 sts).
Round 32a: (Dc in next dc, dc2tog) to end. (8 sts).
Round 33a: (Dc2tog) to end. (4 sts).
Fasten off the work. Break off the yarn, leaving a tail for sewing. Thread the end through rem sts, then pull tight and secure with a knot. Hide the tail of the yarn (see page 136).

Head B

change to blue for head B

Round 21b: Dc around rem 28 sts of round 20, then join into first stitch. (28 sts).
Rounds 22b-33b: Work as for rounds 22a–33a (but using blue). Finish off as for head A.

Arms

Arm A

start with blue
Note: Stuff gradually as arm length grows.
Round 1: Using magic circle technique – work 8 dc. (8 sts).
Rounds 2–5: Dc to end. (8 sts).
change to red
Rounds 6–7: Dc to end. (8 sts).
change to black
Rounds 8–27: Dc to end. (8 sts).
Fasten off the work. Break off the yarn, leaving a tail for sewing. Sew the arm to the body.

Arm B

start with pink
Note: Stuff gradually as arm length grows.
Round 1: Using magic circle technique – work 8 dc. (8 sts).
Rounds 2–5: Dc to end. (8 sts).
change to black
Rounds 6–7: Dc to end. (8 sts).
change to red
Rounds 8–27: Dc to end. (8 sts).
Fasten off the work. Break off the yarn, leaving a tail for sewing. Sew the arm to the body.

Making up

Knot strands of yarn to form hair on each head (see page 136) and trim to desired length. Weave in any loose ends.

BODY AND HEADS

Round	Stitches	Colour	
1	MC 7	Black	
2	14 (inc 7)	Black	
3	21 (inc 7)	Red	
4	28 (inc 7)	Red	
5	35 (inc 7)	Black	
6	42 (inc 7)	Black	
7	49 (inc 7)	Red	
8	56 (inc 7)	Red	
9-20	56	2 rounds Black	2 rounds Red
21a/b	28 – rejoin to first st	Head A Pink	Head B Blue
22–27a/b	28		
Embroider mouth			
28a/b	24 (dec 4)	Head A Pink	Head B Blue
29a/b	20 (dec 4)		
30a/b	16 (dec 4)		
Sew on eyes, stuff firmly			
31a/b	12 (dec 4)	Head A Pink	Head B Blue
32a/b	8 (dec 4)		
33a/b	4 (dec 4)		

ARM A

Round	Stitches	Colour
1	MC 8	Blue
2–5	8	Blue
6–7	8	Red
8–27	8	Black

ARM B

Round	Stitches	Colour
1	MC 8	Pink
2–5	8	Pink
6–7	8	Black
8–27	8	Red

i'm all of a flutter

CROCHET BAKEMONO [monsters!]

YOU WILL NEED

- Debbie Bliss Cashmerino Aran 55% merino wool 33% microfibre 12% cashmere (98yd/90m per 50g) 25g purple, 25g pink

- 3.5mm (UK9:USE/4) crochet hook

- 2 black buttons (for eyes)

- Small pieces of white felt (for eye shapes and nails)

- Embroidery thread (black for nose, white for sewing on button eyes)

- Polyester stuffing

Jinkou

Head

start with purple

Round 1: Using magic circle technique – work 5 dc. (5 sts).
Round 2: (2dc) into each st. (10 sts).
Round 3: (2dc in next dc, dc in next dc) to end. (15 sts).
Round 4: (2dc in next dc, dc in next 2 dc) to end. (20 sts).
Round 5: (2dc in next dc, dc in next 3 dc) to end. (25 sts).
Round 6: (2dc in next dc, dc in next 4 dc) to end. (30 sts).
Round 7: (2dc in next dc, dc in next 5 dc) to end. (35 sts).
Rounds 8–13: Dc to end. (35 sts).

change to pink

Rounds 14–16: Dc to end. (35 sts).

change to purple

Rounds 17–23: Dc to end. (35 sts).

Sew one eye onto the head on top of the felt eye shape with white embroidery thread.

Round 24: (Dc in next 5 dc, dc2tog) to end. (30 sts).
Round 25: (Dc in next 4 dc, dc2tog) to end. (25 sts).

Embroider the nose with black embroidery thread using running stitch.

Round 26: (Dc in next 3 dc, dc2tog) to end. (20 sts).

Sew the second eye onto the head on top of the felt eye shape. Partially stuff then continue stuffing as hole closes.

Round 27: (Dc in next 2 dc, dc2tog) to end. (15 sts).
Round 28: (Dc in next dc, dc2tog) to end. (10 sts).
Round 29: (Dc2tog) to end. (5 sts).

Close the hole and hide the tail of the yarn (see page 136).

Arms (make 2 alike)

start with purple

Round 1: Using magic circle technique – work 7 dc. (7 sts).
Round 2: 2 dc into each st. (14 sts).
Rounds 3–6: Dc to end. (14 sts).

Sew the felt shaped claws onto the arms with white embroidery thread using back stitch.

change to pink

Round 7: (Dc2tog, then dc in next 5 dc) to end. (12 sts).
Round 8: (Dc2tog), then dc in next 4 dc) to end. (10 sts).
Rounds 9–13: Dc to end. (10 sts).

Secure the tail of yarn and leave.

Making up

Sew the arms to the head using the tail of yarn. Weave in any loose ends.

HEAD

Round	Stitches	Colour
1	MC 5	Purple
2	10 (inc 5)	Purple
3	15 (inc 5)	Purple
4	20 (inc 5)	Purple
5	25 (inc 5)	Purple
6	30 (inc 5)	Purple
7	35 (inc 5)	Purple
8–13	35	Purple
14–16	35	Pink
17–23	35	Purple
Sew one eye on top of felt eye shape		
24	30 (dec 5)	Purple
25	25 (dec 5)	Purple
26	20 (dec 5)	Purple
Sew on second eye on top of felt eye shape. Embroider nose. Partially stuff; then cont stuffing as hole closes		
27	15 (dec 5)	Purple
28	10 (dec 5)	Purple
29	5 (dec 5)	Purple
Close hole, hide yarn		

ARMS

Round	Stitches	Colour
1	MC 7	Purple
2	14 (inc 7)	Purple
3	14	Purple
Sew on felt shaped claws		
7	12 (dec 2)	Pink
8	10 (dec 2)	Pink
9–13	10	Pink

i hear you

YOU WILL NEED

- Debbie Bliss Cashmerino Aran 55% merino wool 33% microfibre 12% cashmere (98yd/90m per 50g) 40g light blue, 10g dark blue

- 3.5mm (UK9:USE/4) crochet hook

- 2 blue buttons (for eyes)

- Felt (white for eye mask, pink for tongue)

- Embroidery thread (for eye mask and tongue)

- Polyester stuffing

Adoramon

Main body and legs
use light blue

Round 1: Using magic circle technique – work 5 dc. (5 sts).
Round 2: 2dc into each st. (10 sts).
Round 3: (2dc in next dc, dc in next dc) to end. (15 sts).
Round 4: (2dc in next dc, dc in next 2 dc) to end. (20 sts).
Round 5: (2dc in next dc, dc in next 3 dc) to end. (25 sts).
Round 6: (2dc in next dc, dc in next 4 dc) to end. (30 sts).
Round 7: (2dc in next dc, dc in next 5 dc) to end. (35 sts).
Round 8: (2dc in next dc, dc in next 6 dc) to end. (40 sts).
Round 9: (2dc in next dc, dc in next 20 dc) to end. (44 sts).
Rounds 10–14: Dc to end. (44 sts).
Round 15: (2dc in next dc, dc in next 21 dc) to end. (46 sts).
Round 16: (2dc in next dc, dc in next 22 dc) to end. (48 sts).
Round 17: Dc to end. (48 sts).
Round 18: (Dc in next 11 dc, dc2tog) to end. (44 sts).
Round 19: (Dc in next 10 dc, dc2tog) to end. (40 sts).
Round 20: (Dc in next 9 dc, dc2tog) to end. (36 sts).
Round 21: Dc to end. (36 sts).
Round 22: (Dc in next 8 dc, dc2tog) to end. (32 sts).
Rounds 23–25: Dc to end. (32 sts)

Legs
continue in light blue

Round 26a: Dc 16 sts and join to stitch 1.
Sew on the eye mask and button eyes with white embroidery thread using back stitch. Sew on the tongue with pink embroidery thread. Stuff firmly.
Round 27a–28a: Dc to end. (16 sts).
Round 29a: (Dc2tog) to end. (8 sts).
Stuff firmly.
Round 30a: (Dc2tog) to end. (4 sts).
Close the hole and hide the tail of the yarn (see page 136).
Repeat rounds 26a–30a to form Leg B.

Ears (make 2 alike)
use dark blue

Round 1: Using magic circle technique – work 4 dc. (4 sts).
Round 2: 2dc into each st (8 sts).
Round 3: (2dc in next dc, dc in foll dc) to end. (12 sts).
Round 4: (2dc in next dc, dc in foll 2 dc) to end. (16 sts).
Round 5: (2dc in next dc, dc in foll 3 dc) to end. (20 sts).
Round 6: Dc to end. (20 sts).
Round 7: (Dc in next 4 dc, dc2tog) to end. (16 sts).
Rounds 8–9: Dc to end. (16 sts).
Round 10: (Dc in next 3 dc, dc2tog) to end. (12 sts).

Making up
Secure the tail of yarn then use it to sew the ears to the side of the head. Weave in any loose ends.

MAIN BODY AND LEGS

Round	Stitches	Colour
1	MC 5	Light blue
2	10 (inc 5)	Light blue
3	15 (inc 5)	Light blue
4	20 (inc 5)	Light blue
5	25 (inc 5)	Light blue
6	30 (inc 5)	Light blue
7	35 (inc 5)	Light blue
8	40 (inc 5)	Light blue
9	44 (inc 4)	Light blue
10–14	44	Light blue
15	46 (inc 2)	Light blue
16	48 (inc 2)	Light blue
17	48	Light blue
18	44 (dec 4)	Light blue
19	40 (dec 4)	Light blue
20	36 (dec 4)	Light blue
21	36	Light blue
22	32 (dec 4)	Light blue
23–25	32	Light blue
Form legs		
26a/b	16 (join to st 1)	Light blue
Sew on eye mask and buttons and tongue		
Stuff		
27a/b–28a/b	16	Light blue
29a/b	8 (dec 8)	Light blue
Stuff firmly		
30a/b	4 (dec 4)	Light blue
Close hole, hide tail		

EARS

Round	Stitches	Colour
1	MC 4	Dark blue
2	8 (inc 4)	Dark blue
3	12 (inc 4)	Dark blue
4	16 (inc 4)	Dark blue
5	20 (inc 4)	Dark blue
6	20	Dark blue
7	16 (dec 4)	Dark blue
8–9	16	Dark blue
10	12 (dec 4)	Dark blue

CROCHET BAKEMONO [monsters!]

YOU WILL NEED

- Debbie Bliss Cashmerino Aran 55% merino wool 33% microfibre 12% cashmere (98yd/90m per 50g) 50g grey, 15g yellow, 15g black

- 3.5mm (UK9:USE/4) crochet hook

- 2 blue buttons (for eyes)

- Small piece of white felt (for teeth)

- Embroidery thread (yellow for eyes, white for teeth)

- Polyester stuffing

Takomon

Head and base

start with grey

Round 1: Using magic circle technique – work 6 dc. (6 sts).
Round 2: 2 dc into each st. (12 sts).
Round 3: (2dc in next dc, dc in next dc) to end. (18 sts).
Round 4: (2dc in next dc, dc in next 2 dc) to end. (24 sts).
Round 5: (2dc in next dc, dc in next 3 dc) to end. (30 sts).
Round 6: (2dc in next dc, dc in next 4 dc) to end. (36 sts).
Round 7: (2dc in next dc, dc in next 8 dc) to end. (40 sts).
Round 8: Dc around. (40 sts).
Round 9: (2dc in next dc, dc in next 9 dc) to end. (44 sts).
Rounds 10–18: Dc to end. (44 sts).

change to yellow

Rounds 19–24: Dc to end. (44 sts).
Sew on the button eyes with yellow embroidery thread and felt teeth with white embroidery thread using back stitch.

change to grey

Rounds 25–32: Dc to end. (44 sts).
Round 33: Working into back loops this round only, dc into each st. (44 sts).
Round 34: (Dc in next 9 dc, dc2tog) to end. (40 sts).
Round 35: (Dc in next 8 dc, dc2tog) to end. (35 sts).
Round 36: (Dc in next 7 dc, dc2tog) to end. (30 sts).
Stuff the head firmly, and continue to stuff as the hole closes.
Round 37: (Dc in next 6 dc, dc2tog) to end. (24 sts).
Round 38: (Dc2tog) to end. (12 sts).
Round 39: (Dc2tog) to end. (6 sts).
Round 40: (Dc2tog) to end. (3 sts).
Close the hole and hide the tail of the yarn (see page 136).

Base and tutu

use grey

Round 1: Chain loosely approx 1.5 times the circumference of the head.
Round 2: Chain 2 into each stitch.
Round 3: (Dc 1 st, then dc 2 into next st) to end.
Round 4: Chain 2 into each stitch.
Stitch to the base of the head.
Note: you should be able to wrap the tutu around twice, to form two rounds.

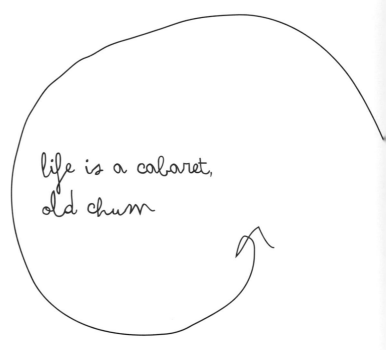

life is a cabaret, old chum

Hat

use black

Round 1: Using magic circle technique – work 5 dc. (5 sts).
Round 2: 2dc into each st. (10 sts).
Round 3: 2dc into each st. (20 sts).
Round 4: (2dc in next dc, dc into next st) to end. (30 sts).
Round 5: Dc to end. (30 sts).
Round 6: Working into back loops this round only, dc into each st. (30 sts).
Rounds 7–12: Dc to end. (30 sts).
Round 13: Working into front loops this round only, 2dc into each st. (60 sts).
Round 14: Dc to end. (60 sts).

Making up

Hide the tail of the yarn (see page 136). Sew the hat to the head then weave in any loose ends.

HEAD AND BASE

Round	Stitches	Colour
1	MC 6	Grey
2	12 (inc 6)	Grey
3	18 (inc 6)	Grey
4	24 (inc 6)	Grey
5	30 (inc 6)	Grey
6	36 (inc 6)	Grey
7	40 (inc 4)	Grey
8	40	Grey
9	44 (inc 4)	Grey
10–18	44	Grey
Change to yellow		
19–24	44	Yellow
Change to grey		
25-32	44	Grey
33	44	Grey
34	40 (dec 4)	Grey
35	35 (dec 5)	Grey
36	30 (dec 5)	Grey
Stuff head firmly and continue to stuff as hole closes		
37	24 (dec 6)	Grey
38	12 (dec 12)	Grey
39	6 (dec 6)	Grey
40	3 (dec 3)	Grey

HAT

Round	Stitches	Colour
1	MC 5	Black
2	10 (inc 5)	Black
3	20 (inc 10)	Black
4	30 (inc 10)	Black
5	30	Black
6	Into back loops 30	Black
7–12	30	Black
13	Into front loops 60 (inc 30)	Black
14	60	Black

where did i leave my ukulele?

 CROCHET BAKEMONO [monsters!]

YOU WILL NEED

- Debbie Bliss Cashmerino Aran 55% merino wool 33% microfibre 12% cashmere (98yd/90m per 50g) 50g green, 15g orange, 10g red

- 3.5mm (UK9:USE/4) crochet hook

- 2 yellow buttons (for eyes)

- Small piece of felt (red for eye mask)

- Embroidery thread (black for eyes, eyebrows and mouth)

- Polyester stuffing

Hulahulamon

Body

use green

Round 1: Using magic circle technique – work 5 dc. (5 sts).
Round 2: 2dc into each st. (10 sts).
Round 3: (2dc in next dc, dc in next dc) to end. (15 sts).
Round 4: (2dc in next dc, dc in next 2 dc) to end. (20 sts).
Round 5: (2dc in next dc, dc in next 3 dc) to end. (25 sts).
Round 6: (2dc in next dc, dc in next 4 dc) to end. (30 sts).
Round 7: (2dc in next dc, dc in next 5 dc) to end. (35 sts).
Round 8: (2dc in next dc, dc in next 6dc) to end. (40 sts).
Round 9: (2dc in next dc, dc in next 7dc) to end. (45 sts).
Round 10: Dc to end. (45 sts).
Round 11: (2dc in next dc, dc in next 8 dc) to end. (50 sts).
Rounds 12–16: Dc to end. (50 sts).
Round 17: (Dc in next 8 dc, dc2tog) to end. (45 sts).
Round 18: Dc to end. (45 sts).
Round 19: (Dc in next 7 dc, dc2tog) to end. (40 sts).
Round 20: (Dc in next 6 dc, dc2tog) to end. (35 sts).
Round 21: (Dc in next 5 dc, dc2tog) to end. (30 sts).
Round 22: (Dc in next 4 dc, dc2tog) to end. (25 sts).
Round 23: Dc to end. (25 sts).
Fill the body with stuffing up to this point (the neck), where the head will be sewn on later.

Skirt

use orange

Weave orange yarn around the waist leaving loops of about 1¹/₂in (4cm). Go all the way around the body part and trim loops to the desired skirt length.
Optional: to make it a child-friendly toy, knot the strands to secure in place.

Head

use green

Round 1: Using magic circle technique – work 5 dc. (5 sts).
Round 2: 2 dc into each st. (10 sts).
Round 3: (2dc in next dc, dc in next dc) to end. (15 sts).
Round 4: (2dc in next dc, dc in next 2 dc) to end. (20 sts).
Round 5: (2dc in next dc, dc in next 3 dc) to end. (25 sts).
Round 6: (2dc in next dc, dc in next 4 dc) to end. (30 sts).
Round 7: Dc to end. (30 sts).
Round 8: (Dc in next 4 dc, dc2tog) to end. (25 sts).
Rounds 9–12: Dc to end. (25 sts).

Interim finishing

Sew on the eyes, eye mask, mouth and eyebrows with black embroidery thread. Stuff the head and sew onto the body.

Arms (make 2 alike)

start with red

Round 1: Using magic circle technique – work 5 dc. (5 sts).
Round 2: 2 dc into each st. (10 sts).
Rounds 3–5: Dc to end. (10 sts).
change to green
Rounds 6–10: Dc to end. (10 sts).

Legs (make 2 alike)

use red

Round 1: Using magic circle technique – work 6 dc. (6 sts).
Round 2: 2 dc into each st. (12 sts).
Rounds 3–5: Dc to end. (12 sts).

Making up

Sew the arms and legs to the body. Weave in any loose ends.

BODY

Round	Stitches	Colour
1	MC 5	Green
2	10 (inc 5)	Green
3	15 (inc 5)	Green
4	20 (inc 5)	Green
5	25 (inc 5)	Green
6	30 (inc 5)	Green
7	35 (inc 5)	Green
8	40 (inc 5)	Green
9	45 (inc 5)	Green
10	45	Green
11	50 (inc 5)	Green
12–16	50	Green
17	45 (dec 5)	Green
18	45	Green
19	40 (dec 5)	Green
20	35 (dec 5)	Green
21	30 (dec 5)	Green
22	25 (dec 5)	Green
23	25	Green

HEAD

Round	Stitches	Colour
1	MC 5	Green
2	10 (inc 5)	Green
3	15 (inc 5)	Green
4	20 (inc 5)	Green
5	25 (inc 5)	Green
6	30 (inc 5)	Green
7	30	Green
8	25 (dec 5)	Green
9–12	25	Green

ARMS

Round	Stitches	Colour
1	MC 5	Red
2	10 (inc 5)	Red
3–5	10	Red
6–10	10	Green

LEGS

Round	Stitches	Colour
1	MC 6	Red
2	12 (inc 6)	Red
3–5	12	Red

hogaraga, practises his dancing steps

CROCHET BAKEMONO [monsters!]

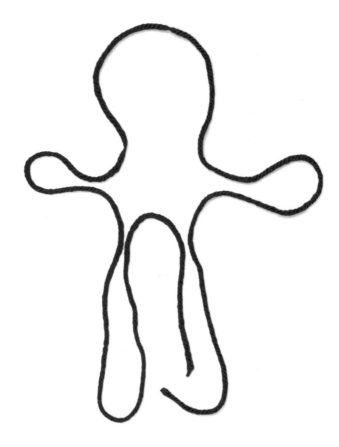

YOU WILL NEED

- Debbie Bliss Cashmerino Aran 55% merino wool 33% microfibre
  12% cashmere (98yd/90m per 50g)
  50g blue, 10g red, 10g orange, 10g yellow,
  10g green, 10g pink

- 3.5mm (UK9:USE/4) crochet hook

- 2 blue buttons (for eyes)

- Small pieces of felt (light pink for face
  and dark pink for mouth)

- Embroidery thread (blue for face, white for toes)

- Polyester stuffing

Hogaraga

Body

use blue

Round 1: Using magic circle technique – work 5 dc. (5 sts).
Round 2: 2dc into each st. (10 sts).
Round 3: (2dc in next dc, dc in next dc) to end. (15 sts).
Round 4: (2dc in next dc, dc in next 2 dc) to end. (20 sts).
Round 5: (2dc in next dc, dc in next 3 dc) to end. (25 sts).
Round 6: (2dc in next dc, dc in next 4 dc) to end. (30 sts).
Round 7: (2dc in next dc, dc in next 5 dc) to end. (35 sts).
Round 8: (2dc in next dc, dc in next 6 dc) to end. (40 sts).
Round 9: Dc to end. (40 sts).
Round 10: (2dc in next dc, dc in next 9 dc) to end. (44 sts).
Round 11: Dc to end. (44 sts).
Round 12: (2dc in next dc, dc in next 10 dc) to end. (48 sts).
Rounds 13–21: Dc to end. (48 sts).
Round 22: (Dc in next 22 dc, dc2tog) to end. (46 sts).
Round 23: Dc to end. (46 sts).
Round 24: Dc2tog once, then to end. (45 sts).
Round 25: (Dc in next 7 dc, dc2tog) to end. (40 sts).
Round 26: (Dc in next 3 dc, dc2tog) to end. (32 sts).
Break off the yarn. Fasten off the work, leaving a tail for sewing.
Sew on the eyes with blue embroidery thread and embroider the
face and mouth using darned lines.
Stuff the body firmly.
Round 27: (Dc in next 2dc, dc2tog) to end. (24 sts).
Round 28: (Dc in next 2dc, dc2tog) to end. (18 sts).
Round 29: (Dc2tog) to end. (9 sts).
Round 30: Dc in first st, then (dc2tog) to end. (5 sts).
Close the hole and hide the tail of the yarn (see page 136).

Legs (make 2 alike)

Note: Stuff the leg lightly as it is formed.
start with blue

Round 1: Using magic circle technique – work 4 dc. (4 sts).
Round 2: 2dc into each st. (8 sts).
Round 3: (2dc in next dc, dc in next dc) to end. (12 sts).
Round 4: (2dc in next dc, dc in next 5 dc) to end. (14 sts).
Rounds 5–6: Dc to end. (14 sts).
Round 7: (Dc in next 5dc, dc2tog) to end. (12 sts).
Round 8: (Dc in next 4dc, dc2tog) to end. (10 sts).
Round 9: Dc to end. (10 sts).
Round 10: (Dc in next 3 dc, dc2tog) to end. (8 sts).
Embroider on the toes with white embroidery thread using darned
lines. Stuff the piece and continue to stuff as the leg lengthens.
Rounds 11–13: (Dc to end) in red.
Rounds 14–16: (Dc to end) in orange.
Rounds 17–19: (Dc to end) in yellow.
Rounds 20–22: (Dc to end) in green.
Rounds 23–25: (Dc to end) in blue.
Once the blue rounds have been worked, just fasten off and sew
to the base of the body.

Arms (make 2 alike)

Note: Stuff the arm lightly as it is formed.
start with pink

Round 1: Using magic circle technique – work 4 dc. (4 sts).
Round 2: 2dc into each st. (8 sts).
Rounds 3–6: Dc to end. (8 sts).
change to blue
Rounds 7–20: Dc to end. (8 sts).
Break off the yarn. Fasten off the work, leaving a tail for sewing.
Sew the arms in place on the body.

Making up

Sew in any loose ends.

BODY

Round	Stitches	Colour
1	MC 5	Blue
2	10 (inc 5)	Blue
3	15 (inc 5)	Blue
4	20 (inc 5)	Blue
5	25 (inc 5)	Blue
6	30 (inc 5)	Blue
7	35 (inc 5)	Blue
8	40 (inc 5)	Blue
9	40	Blue
10	44 (inc 4)	Blue
11	44	Blue
12	48 (inc 4)	Blue
13–21	48	Blue
22	46 (dec 2)	Blue
23	46	Blue
24	45 (dec 1)	Blue
25	40 (dec 5)	Blue
26	32 (dec 8)	Blue
Sew on face, eyes and mouth		
Stuff firmly		
27	24 (dec 8)	Blue
28	18 (dec 6)	Blue
29	9 (dec 9)	Blue
30	4 (dec 5)	Blue

LEGS

Round	Stitches	Colour
1	MC 4	Blue
2	8 (inc 4)	Blue
3	12 (inc 4)	Blue
4	14 (inc 2)	Blue
5–6	14	Blue
7	12 (dec 2)	Blue
8	10 (dec 2)	Blue
9	10	Blue
10	8 (dec 2)	Blue
Embroider on toes		
Stuff as leg continues to lengthen		
11–13	8	Red
14–16	8	Orange
17–19	8	Yellow
20–22	8	Green
23–25	8	Blue

ARMS

Round	Stitches	Colour
1	MC 4	Pink
2	8 (inc 4)	Pink
3–6	8	Pink
7–20	8	Blue

CROCHET BAKEMONO [monsters!]

teeth were important from the very start

YOU WILL NEED

- Debbie Bliss Cashmerino Aran 55% merino wool 33% microfibre 12% cashmere (98yd/90m per 50g) 50g pink

- 3.5mm (UK9:USE/4) crochet hook

- 1 large black button and 1 small yellow button (for eye)

- Small pieces of felt (white for brow and teeth, and yellow for nails and mouth)

- Embroidery thread (black for sewing on the button eyes, pink for felt details)

- Polyester stuffing

Mokumon

Head and body
use pink

Round 1: Using magic circle technique – work 6 dc. (6 sts).
Round 2: 2dc into each st. (12 sts).
Round 3: (2dc in next dc, dc in next dc) to end. (18 sts).
Round 4: (2dc in next dc, dc in next 2 dc) to end. (24 sts).
Round 5: (2dc in next dc, dc in next 3 dc) to end. (30 sts).
Round 6: (2dc in next dc, dc in next 4 dc) to end. (36 sts).
Round 7: (2dc in next dc, dc in next 5 dc) to end. (42 sts).
Round 8: (2dc in next dc, dc in next 6 dc) to end. (48 sts).
Rounds 9–19: Dc around. (48 sts).
Round 20: (Dc in next 22 dc, dc2tog) to end. (46 sts).
Rounds 21–23: Dc to end. (46 sts).
Round 24: (Dc in next 21 dc, dc2tog) to end. (44 sts).
Round 25: Dc to end. (44 sts).
Round 26: (Dc in next 20 dc, dc2tog) to end. (42 sts).
Round 27: Dc to end. (42 sts).
Round 28: (Dc in next 19 dc, dc2tog) to end. (40 sts).
Round 29: Dc to end. (40 sts).
Round 30: (Dc in next 18 dc, dc2tog) to end. (38 sts).
Round 31: Dc to end. (38 sts).
Round 32: (Dc in next 17 dc, dc2tog) to end. (36 sts).
Round 33: Dc around. (36 sts).
Partially stuff.
Continue from here to begin the legs.

Legs
Leg A (bigger leg)
continue in pink

Round 34a: Dc around 24 sts, then join into first st. (24 sts).
Sew on the eye buttons with black embroidery thread and the white and yellow felt for the brow, teeth and mouth with pink embroidery thread using back stitch.
Round 35a: Dc around. (24 sts).
Round 36a: (Dc in net dc, dc2tog) to end. (18 sts).
Round 37a: (Dc in next dc, dc2tog) to end. (12 sts).
Stuff the whole piece firmly.
Round 38a: (Dc2tog) to end. (6 sts).
Round 39a: (Dc2tog) to end. (3 sts).
Fasten off the work. Break off the yarn, leaving a tail for sewing. Close the hole and hide the tail of the yarn (see page 136).

Leg B (smaller leg)
continue in pink

Round 34b: Dc around rem 12 sts, then join into first st. (12 sts).
Round 35b: Dc to end. (12 sts).
Round 36b: (Dc in next 4 dc, dc2tog) to end. (10 sts).
Round 37b: (Dc in next 3 dc, dc2tog) to end. (8 sts).
Stuff the leg firmly.
Round 38b: (Dc in next 2 dc, dc2tog) to end. (6 sts).
Round 39b: (Dc2tog) to end. (3 sts).
Fasten off the work. Break off the yarn, leaving a tail for sewing. Close the hole and hide the tail of the yarn (see page 136).

Arms (make 2 alike)
use pink

Round 1: Using magic circle technique – work 4 dc. (4 sts).
Round 2: 2dc into each st. (8 sts).
Rounds 3–7: Dc to end. (8 sts).

Making up
Sew on the felt nails with pink embroidery thread using back stitch and lightly stuff the arms, then sew the arms to the body. Weave in any loose ends.

HEAD AND BODY

Round	Stitches	Colour
1	MC 6	Pink
2	12 (inc 6)	Pink
3	18 (inc 6)	Pink
4	24 (inc 6)	Pink
5	30 (inc 6)	Pink
6	36 (inc 6)	Pink
7	42 (inc 6)	Pink
8	48 (inc 6)	Pink
9–19	48	Pink
20	46 (dec 2)	Pink
21–23	46	Pink
24	44 (dec 2)	Pink
25	44	Pink
26	42 (dec 2)	Pink
27	42	Pink
28	40 (dec 2)	Pink
29	40	Pink
30	38 (dec 2)	Pink
31	38	Pink
32	36 (dec 2)	Pink
33	36	Pink
Partially stuff		
Form legs		

LEGS

Round	Stitches	Colour
Leg A		
34a	24 – rejoin to first st	Pink
Sew on eye buttons, brow, teeth, mouth and nails		
35a	24	Pink
36a	18 (dec 6)	Pink
37a	12 (dec 6)	Pink
Stuff leg		
38a	6 (dec 6)	Pink
39a	3 (dec 3)	Pink
Leg B		
34b	12 (rejoin to first st)	Pink
35b	12 (dec 2)	Pink
36b	10 (dec 2)	Pink
37b	8 (dec 2)	Pink
Stuff leg		
38b	6 (dec 2)	Pink
39b	3 (dec 3)	Pink

ARMS

Round	Stitches	Colour
1	MC 4	Pink
2	8 (inc 4)	Pink
3–7	8	Pink

all the better to see you with

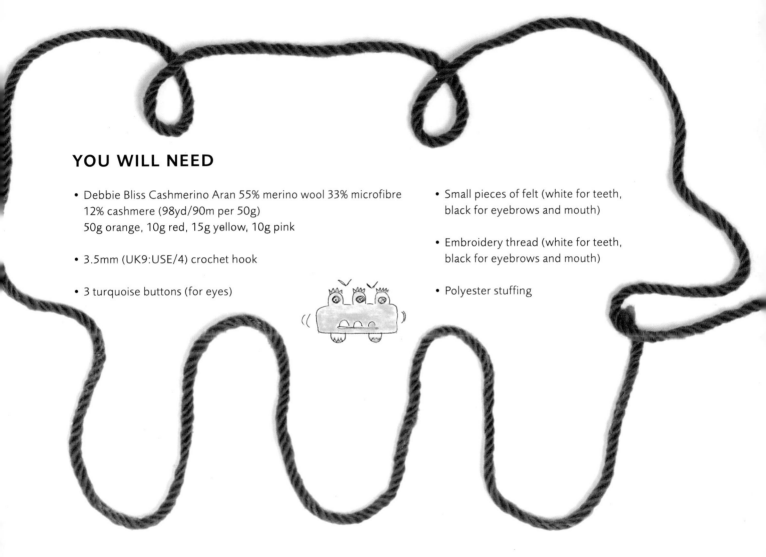

YOU WILL NEED

- Debbie Bliss Cashmerino Aran 55% merino wool 33% microfibre 12% cashmere (98yd/90m per 50g) 50g orange, 10g red, 15g yellow, 10g pink

- 3.5mm (UK9:USE/4) crochet hook

- 3 turquoise buttons (for eyes)

- Small pieces of felt (white for teeth, black for eyebrows and mouth)

- Embroidery thread (white for teeth, black for eyebrows and mouth)

- Polyester stuffing

Kitsu

Eye backings

make 1 each in red, yellow and pink

Round 1: Using magic circle technique – work 5 dc. (5 sts).
Round 2: 2dc into each st. (10 sts).
Round 3: (2dc in next dc, dc in next 4 dc) to end. (12 sts).
Rounds 4–10: Dc to end. (12 sts).
Fasten off the work. Break off the yarn, leaving a tail for sewing. Sew on one button eye to each eye backing using orange yarn. Stuff the backings firmly.

Head

use orange

Round 1: Using magic circle technique – work 6 dc. (6 sts).
Round 2: 2dc into each st. (12 sts).
Round 3: (2dc in next dc, dc in next dc) to end. (18 sts).
Round 4: (2dc in next dc, dc in next 2 dc) to end. (24 sts).
Round 5: (2dc in next dc, dc in next 3 dc) to end. (30 sts).
Round 6: (2dc in next dc, dc in next 4 dc) to end. (36 sts).
Round 7: Dc to end. (36 sts).
Round 8: (2dc in next dc, dc in next 17 dc) to end. (38 sts).
Rounds 9–27: Dc around. (38 sts).
Round 28: (Dc in next 17 dc, dc2tog) to end. (36 sts).
Round 29: Dc to end. (36 sts).
Round 30: (Dc in next 4 dc, dc2tog) to end. (30 sts).
Round 31: (Dc in next 3 dc, dc2tog) to end. (24 sts).
Stuff the head firmly.
Round 32: (Dc in next 2 dc, dc2tog) to end. (18 sts).
Round 33: (Dc in next dc, dc2tog) to end. (12 sts).
Round 34: (Dc2tog) to end. (6 sts).
Fasten off the work. Break off the yarn, leaving a tail for sewing. Thread the end through rem sts, then pull tight and secure with a knot. Hide the tail of the yarn (see page 136).
Sew the yellow eye backing to the middle of the head piece and sew the red and pink eye backings to either side of the yellow one with matching yarns.
Sew on the felt mouth and eyebrows with black embroidery thread and the teeth with white embroidery thread using running stitch.

Feet (make 4)

start with yellow

Round 1: Using magic circle technique – work 6 dc. (6 sts).
Round 2: 2dc into each st. (12 sts).
Round 3: (2dc in next dc, dc in next dc) to end. (18 sts).
change to orange
Round 4: (Dc in next dc, dc2tog) to end. (12 sts).
Rounds 5–6: Dc to end. (12 sts).
Fasten off the work. Break off the yarn, leaving a tail for sewing. Thread the end through rem sts, then pull tight and secure with a knot. Hide the tail of the yarn (see page 136). Stuff the feet firmly and sew them to the head.

Making up

Weave in any loose ends.

EYE BACKINGS

Round	Stitches	Colour
1	MC 5	Red/Yellow/Pink
2	10 (inc 5)	Red/Yellow/Pink
3	12 (inc 2)	Red/Yellow/Pink
4–10	12	Red/Yellow/Pink

HEAD

Round	Stitches	Colour
1	MC 6	Orange
2	12 (inc 6)	Orange
3	18 (inc 6)	Orange
4	24 (inc 6)	Orange
5	30 (inc 6)	Orange
6	36 (inc 6)	Orange
7	36	Orange
8	38 (inc 2)	Orange
9–27	38	Orange
28	36 (dec 2)	Orange
29	36	Orange
30	30 (dec 6)	Orange
31	24 (dec 6)	Orange
Stuff firmly		
32	18 (dec 6)	Orange
33	12 (dec 6)	Orange
34	6 (dec 6)	Orange

FEET

Round	Stitches	Colour
1	MC 6	Yellow
2	12 (inc 6)	Yellow
3	18 (inc 6)	Yellow
4	12 (dec 6)	Orange
5–6	12	Orange

three eyes, four feet and an extraordinary figure – that's what we call unusual

bouncy
bouncy
bouncy

CROCHET BAKEMONO [monsters!]

YOU WILL NEED

• Debbie Bliss Cashmerino Aran 55% merino wool
  33% microfibre 12% cashmere (98yd/90m per 50g)
  25g white, 25g red, 10g blue

• 3.5mm (UK9:USE/4) crochet hook

• 2 blue buttons (for eyes)

• Small pieces of felt (red for eyelashes, white for teeth)

• Embroidery thread (white for teeth)

• Polyester stuffing

Pakkumamon

Bottom head

start with white

Round 1: Using magic circle technique – work 5 dc. (5 sts).
Round 2: 2dc into each st. (10 sts).
Round 3: (2dc in next dc, dc in next dc) to end. (15 sts).
Round 4: (2dc in next dc, dc in next 2 dc) to end. (20 sts).
Round 5: (2dc in next dc, dc in next 3 dc) to end. (25 sts).
Round 6: (2dc in next dc, dc in next 4 dc) to end. (30 sts).
Round 7: (2dc in next dc, dc in next 5 dc) to end. (35 sts).
Round 8: (2dc in next dc, dc in next 6 dc) to end. (40 sts).
Round 9: Dc to end. (40 sts).
Round 10: (2dc in next dc, dc in next 7 dc) to end. (45 sts).
Rounds 11–12: Dc to end. (45 sts).

change to blue

Round 13: Dc to end. (45 sts).

change to red

Round 14: Working through back loops for this round only, (dc in next 7 dc, dc2tog) to end. (40 sts).
Round 15: (Dc in next 2 dc, dc2tog) to end. (30 sts).
Round 16: (Dc in next 4 dc, dc2tog) to end. (25 sts).
Round 17: (Dc in next 3 dc, dc2tog) to end. (20 sts).
Round 18: (Dc2tog) to end. (10 sts).
Lightly stuff the bottom head.
Round 19: (Dc2tog) to end. (5 sts).
Fasten off the work. Break off the yarn, leaving a tail for sewing. Thread the end through rem sts, then pull tight and secure with a knot. Hide the tail of the yarn (see page 136).

Top head

start with white

Round 1: Using magic circle technique – work 5 dc. (5 sts).
Round 2: 2 dc into each st. (10 sts).
Round 3: (2dc in next dc, dc in next dc) to end. (15 sts).
Round 4: (2dc in next dc, dc in next 2 dc) to end. (20 sts).
Round 5: (2dc in next dc, dc in next 3 dc) to end. (25 sts).
Round 6: (2dc in next dc, dc in next 4 dc) to end. (30 sts).
Round 7: (2dc in next dc, dc in next 5 dc) to end. (35 sts).
Round 8: (2dc in next dc, dc in next 6 dc) to end. (40 sts).
Round 9: Dc to end. (40 sts).
Round 10: (2dc in next dc, dc in next 7 dc) to end. (45 sts).
Rounds 11–13: Dc to end. (45 sts).

change to blue

Round 14: Dc to end. (45 sts).

change to red

Round 15: Working into back loops for this round only, (dc in next 7 dc, dc2tog) to end. (40 sts).
Round 16: (Dc in next 2 dc, dc2tog) to end. (30 sts).
Round 17: (Dc in next 4 dc, dc2tog) to end. (25 sts).
Round 18: (Dc in next 3 dc, dc2tog) to end. (20 sts).
Sew on the button eyes and red felt eyelashes using the white yarn.
Round 19: (Dc2tog) to end. (10 sts).
Lightly stuff the top head.
Round 20: (dc2tog) to end. (5 sts).
Fasten off the work. Break off the yarn, leaving a tail for sewing. Thread the end through rem sts, then pull tight and secure with a knot. Hide the tail of the yarn (see page 136).

Making up

Stitch the bottom and top head together using blue yarn with about 15 blanket stitches (see page 136). Sew on the felt teeth using white embroidery thread. Weave in any loose ends.

hand over the cake!

BOTTOM HEAD		
Round	Stitches	Colour
1	MC 5	White
2	10 (inc 5)	White
3	15 (inc 5)	White
4	20 (inc 5)	White
5	25 (inc 5)	White
6	30 (inc 5)	White
7	35 (inc 5)	White
8	40 (inc 5)	White
9	40	White
10	45 (inc 5)	White
11–12	45	White
13	45	Blue
14	Into back loops 40 (dec 5)	Red
15	30 (dec 10)	Red
16	25 (dec 5)	Red
17	20 (dec 5)	Red
18	10 (dec 10)	Red
Lightly stuff		
19	5 (dec 5)	Red
Lightly stuff		

TOP HEAD		
Round	Stitches	Colour
1	MC 5	White
2	10 (inc 5)	White
3	15 (inc 5)	White
4	20 (inc 5)	White
5	25 (inc 5)	White
6	30 (inc 5)	White
7	35 (inc 5)	White
8	40 (inc 5)	White
9	40	White
10	45 (inc 5)	White
11–13	45	White
14	45	Blue
15	Into back loops 40 (dec 5)	Red
16	30 (dec 10)	Red
17	25 (dec 5)	Red
18	20 (dec 5)	Red
Sew on eyes and eyelashes		
19	10 (dec 10)	Red
Lightly stuff		
20	5 (dec 5)	Red

we have lift off

YOU WILL NEED

- Debbie Bliss Cashmerino Aran 55% merino wool 33% microfibre 12% cashmere (98yd/90m per 50g) 50g blue, 20g red, 20g white

- 3.5mm (UK9:USE/4) crochet hook

- 1 large and 1 small red button (for eyes)

- Small piece of white felt (for eye backings, mouth and teeth)

- Embroidery thread (blue for mouth)

- Polyester stuffing

Rokemono

101

Body
start with red
Round 1: Using magic circle technique – work 4 dc. (4 sts).
Round 2: 2dc into each st. (8 sts).
Round 3: (2dc in next dc, dc in next dc) to end. (12 sts).
Round 4: (2dc in next dc, dc in next 3 dc) to end. (15 sts).
Round 5: (2dc in next dc, dc in next 2 dc) to end. (20 sts).
change to white
Round 6: (2dc in next dc, dc in next 3 dc) to end. (25 sts).
Round 7: (2dc in next dc, dc in next 4 dc) to end. (30 sts).
change to blue
Round 8: (2dc in next dc, dc in next 9 dc) to end. (33 sts).
Round 9: (2dc in next dc, dc in next 10 dc) to end. (36 sts).
Rounds 10–11: Dc to end. (36 sts).
change to white
Round 12: (2dc in next dc, dc in next 17 dc) to end. (38 sts).
change to red
Round 13: Dc to end. (38 sts).
change to white
Round 14: Dc to end. (38 sts).
change to blue
Rounds 15–24: Dc to end. (38 sts).
change to red
Rounds 25–26: Dc to end. (38 sts).
change to white
Round 27: Dc to end. (38 sts).
change to red
Rounds 28–29: Dc to end. (38 sts).
Sew on the felt eye backings and button eyes, then sew on the felt mouth with blue embroidery thread using running stitch.

change to white
Rounds 30–35: Dc to end. (38 sts).
Round 36: (Dc in next 17 dc, dc2tog) to end. (36 sts).
Stuff the body firmly.
Round 37: (Dc in next 2 dc, dc2tog) to end. (27 sts).
Round 38: (Dc in next dc, dc2tog) to end. (18 sts).
Round 39: (Dc2tog) to end. (9 sts).
Round 40: Dc in next dc, (dc2tog to end). (5 sts).
Fasten off the work. Break off the yarn, leaving a tail for sewing. Thread the end through rem sts, then pull tight and secure with a knot. Hide the tail of the yarn (see page 136).

Blades (make 4)
start with blue
Round 1: Using magic circle technique – work 5 dc. (5 sts).
Round 2: 2dc into each st. (10 sts).
Round 3: (2dc in next dc, dc in next dc) to end. (15 sts).
Rounds 4–5: Dc to end. (15 sts).
change to red
Rounds 6–7: Dc to end. (15 sts).
Fasten off the work. Break off the yarn, leaving a tail for sewing. Stuff the blades, and sew to the base of the body.

Making up
Weave in any loose ends.

BODY

Round	Stitches	Colour
1	MC 4	Red
2	8 (inc 4)	Red
3	12 (inc 4)	Red
4	15 (inc 3)	Red
5	20 (inc 5)	Red
6	25 (inc 5)	White
7	30 (inc 5)	White
8	33 (inc 3)	Blue
9	36 (inc 3)	Blue
10–11	36	Blue
12	38 (inc 2)	White
13	38	Red
14	38	White
15–24	38	Blue
25–26	38	Red
27	38	White
28–29	38	Red
Sew on felt eye backings, button eyes and mouth		
30–35	38	White
36	36 (dec 2)	White
Stuff firmly		
37	27 (dec 9)	White
38	18 (dec 9)	White
39	9 (dec 9)	White
40	2 into 1	White

BLADES

Round	Stitches	Colour
1	MC 5	Blue
2	10 (inc 5)	Blue
3	15 (inc 5)	Blue
4–5	15	Blue
6–7	15	Red

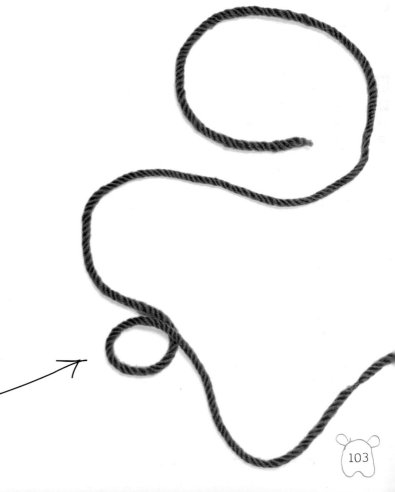

rocket fuel

103

want a hug?

CROCHET BAKEMONO [monsters!]

YOU WILL NEED

- Debbie Bliss Cashmerino Aran 55% merino wool 33% microfibre 12% cashmere (98yd/90m per 50g)
  25g pale blue, 5g purple

- 3.5mm (UK9:USE/4) crochet hook

- Small pieces of felt (purple for face and tummy)

- 2 pale green buttons (for eyes)

- Embroidery thread (pink for mouth, silver for face)

- Polyester stuffing

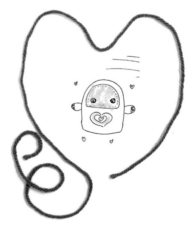

Okaasan

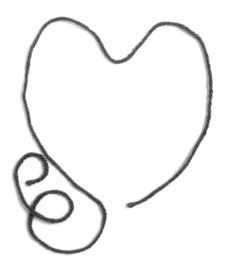

Body

use blue

Round 1: Using magic circle technique – work 5 dc. (5 sts).
Round 2: 2dc into each st. (10 sts).
Round 3: (2dc in next dc, dc in next dc) to end. (15 sts).
Round 4: (2dc in next dc, dc in next 2 dc) to end. (20 sts).
Round 5: (2dc in next dc, dc in next 3 dc) to end. (25 sts).
Round 6: (2dc in next dc, dc in next 4 dc) to end. (30 sts).
Round 7: (2dc in next dc, dc in next 5 dc) to end. (35 sts).
Round 8: (2dc in next dc, dc in next 6 dc) to end. (40 sts).
Round 9: (2dc in next dc, dc in next 19 dc) to end. (42 sts).
Round 10: (2dc in next dc, dc in next 20 dc) to end. (44 sts).
Rounds 11–30: Dc to end. (44 sts).
Sew on the felt face and eyes with silver embroidery thread; then embroider the mouth with pink embroidery thread using back stitch. Sew on the heart tummy with blue yarn using running stitch. Partially stuff the body.
Round 31: Dc to end. (44 sts).
Round 32: Working into back loops only for this round, dc to end. (44 sts).
Round 33: (Dc in next 9 dc, dc2tog) to end. (40 sts).
Round 34: (Dc in next 2 dc, dc2tog) to end. (30 sts).
Round 35: (Dc in next dc, dc2tog) to end. (20 sts).
Round 36: (Dc in next 2 dc, dc2tog) to end. (15 sts).
Stuff the body firmly.

Round 37: (Dc in next dc, dc2tog) to end. (10 sts).
Round 38: (Dc2tog) to end. (5 sts).
Fasten off the work. Break off the yarn, leaving a tail for sewing. Thread the end through rem sts, then pull tight and secure with a knot. Hide the tail of the yarn (see page 136).

Arms (make 2 alike)

start with purple

Round 1: Using magic circle technique – work 5 dc. (5 sts).
Round 2: 2dc into each st. (10 sts).
Round 3: Dc to end. (10 sts).
change to blue
Rounds 4–8: Dc to end. (10 sts).
Stuff both arms lightly and sew one arm to each side of body.

Making up

Weave in any loose ends.

BODY

Round	Stitches	Colour
1	MC 5	Blue
2	10 (inc 5)	Blue
3	15 (inc 5)	Blue
4	20 (inc 5)	Blue
5	25 (inc 5)	Blue
6	30 (inc 5)	Blue
7	35 (inc 5)	Blue
8	40 (inc 5)	Blue
9	42 (inc 2)	Blue
10	44 (inc 2)	Blue
11–30	44	Blue
Sew on felt face, button eyes and heart tummy. Embroider mouth. Partially stuff		
31	44	Blue
32	Into back loops 44	Blue
33	40 (dec 4)	Blue
34	30 (dec 10)	Blue
35	20 (dec 10)	Blue
36	15 (dec 5)	Blue
Stuff firmly		
37	10 (dec 5)	Blue
38	5 (dec 5)	Blue

ARMS

Round	Stitches	Colour
1	MC 5	Purple
2	10 (inc 5)	Purple
3	10	Purple
4–8	10	Blue

107

 CROCHET BAKEMONO [monsters!]

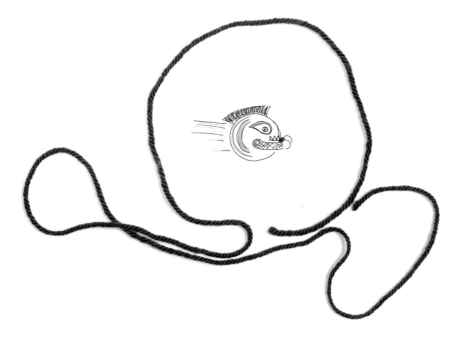

YOU WILL NEED

- Debbie Bliss Cashmerino Aran 55% merino wool
  33% microfibre 12% cashmere (98yd/90m per 50g)
  25g blue, 25g purple, 10g white

- 3.5mm (UK9:USE/4) crochet hook

- 2 black buttons (for eyes)

- Small pieces of felt (purple and blue for teardrop-shaped
  eye backings, white for teeth)

- Embroidery thread (white for teeth,
  purple for button eyes)

- Polyester stuffing

Korobumon

Head pieces (make 2 alike)

start with blue

Round 1: Using magic circle technique – work 5 dc. (5 sts).

Round 2: 2dc into each st. (10 sts).

Round 3: (Dc in next dc, 2dc in next dc) to end. (15 sts).

Round 4: (Dc in next 2 dc, 2dc in next dc) to end. (20 sts).

Round 5: (Dc in next 3 dc, 2dc in next dc) to end. (25 sts).

Round 6: (Dc in next 3 dc, then 2dc in next dc twice) to end. (35 sts).

Round 7: (Dc in next 6 dc, 2dc in next dc) to end. (40 sts).

Round 8: (Dc in next 6 dc, then 2dc in next dc twice) to end. (50 sts).

Round 9: (Dc in next 9 dc, 2dc in next dc) to end. (55 sts).

Round 10: (Dc in next 10 dc, 2dc in next dc) to end. (60 sts).

Round 11: Through back loops only, dc to end. (60 sts).

change to purple

Round 12: Dc to end. (60 sts).

change to blue

Round 13: Dc to end. (60 sts).

change to purple

Round 14: Dc to end. (60 sts).

change to blue

Round 15: Dc to end. (60 sts).

change to purple

Round 16: Dc to end. (60 sts).

Break off the yarn, leaving a blue tail.

Partially sew the two head pieces together (³/₄ of the way round) using the blue tail, then sew on the felt eye backings and button eyes with purple embroidery thread.

Finish sewing the two halves together with the blue tail, stuffing firmly before closing. Sew on the felt teeth with white embroidery thread using running stitch.

Arms (make 2 alike)

start with white

Round 1: Using magic circle technique – work 5 dc. (5 sts).

Round 2: 2dc into each st. (10 sts).

Round 3: (2dc in next dc, dc in next dc) to end. (15 sts).

Round 4: Dc to end. (15 sts).

Round 5: (Dc in next dc, dc2tog) to end. (10 sts).

Round 6: Dc to end. (10 sts).

change to purple

Rounds 7–30: Dc to end. (10 sts).

Sew the arms to the side of head as shown.

If you like, knot 20 x 2in (5cm) lengths of white yarn to the top of the head, to form a Mohican-style hairstyle (see page 136).

Making up

Weave in any loose ends.

HEAD PIECES

Round	Stitches	Colour
1	MC 5	Blue
2	10 (inc 5)	Blue
3	15 (inc 5)	Blue
4	20 (inc 5)	Blue
5	25 (inc 5)	Blue
6	35 (inc 10)	Blue
7	40 (inc 5)	Blue
8	50 (inc 10)	Blue
9	55 (inc 5)	Blue
10	60 (inc 5)	Blue
11	Into back loops 60	Blue
12	60	Purple
13	60	Blue
14	60	Purple
15	60	Blue
16	60	Purple

ARMS

Round	Stitches	Colour
1	MC 5	White
2	10 (inc 5)	White
3	15 (inc 5)	White
4	15	White
5	10 (dec 5)	White
6	10	White
7–30	10	Purple

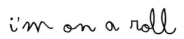

i'm on a roll

aghh!

YOU WILL NEED

- Debbie Bliss Cashmerino Aran 55% merino wool 33% microfibre 12% cashmere (98yd/90m per 50g) 50g pink, 10g white, 10g black

- 3.5mm (UK9:USE/4) crochet hook

- 2 black buttons (for eyes)

- Small pieces of felt (black for mouth, white for sewing on button eyes)

- Embroidery thread (white for sewing on button eyes, black for tummy stitch)

- Polyester stuffing

Kaibutsu

Head

use purple

Round 1: Using magic circle technique – work 5 dc. (5 sts).
Round 2: 2dc into each st. (10 sts).
Round 3: (2dc in next dc, dc in next dc) to end. (15 sts).
Round 4: (2dc in next dc, dc in next 2 dc) to end. (20 sts).
Round 5: (2dc in next dc, dc in next 3 dc) to end. (25 sts).
Round 6: (2dc in next dc, dc in next 4 dc) to end. (30 sts).
Round 7: (2dc in next dc, dc in next 5 dc) to end. (35 sts).
Round 8: (2dc in next dc, dc in next 6 dc) to end. (40 sts).
Round 9: (2dc in next dc, dc in next 9 dc) to end. (44 sts).
Round 10: (2dc in next dc, dc in next 10 dc) to end. (48 sts).
Rounds 11–23: Dc to end. (48 sts).
Round 24: Working into back loops for this round only,
dc to end. (48 sts).
Round 25: (Dc in next 2 dc, dc2tog) to end. (36 sts).
Round 26: (Dc in next 4 dc, dc2tog) to end. (30 sts).
Round 27: (Dc in next dc, dc2tog) to end. (20 sts).
Sew on the button eyes and eyebrow with black embroidery
thread. Embroider a mouth with the yellow yarn as shown.
Stuff the head firmly.
Round 28: (Dc2tog) to end. (10 sts).
Round 29: (Dc2tog) to end. (5 sts).
Fasten off the work. Break off the yarn, leaving a tail for sewing.
Thread the end through rem sts, then pull tight and secure
with a knot. Hide the tail of the yarn (see page 136).

Petals

make 4 orange and 4 yellow
(or enough to alternate around the base of head)

Round 1: Using magic circle technique – work 6 dc. (6 sts).
Round 2: 2dc into each st. (12 sts).
Rounds 3–6: Dc to end. (12 sts).
Fasten off the work. Break off the yarn, leaving a tail for sewing.
Sew the petals to the base of the head.

Making up

Weave in any loose ends.

HEAD

Round	Stitches	Colour
1	MC 5	Purple
2	10 (inc 5)	Purple
3	15 (inc 5)	Purple
4	20 (inc 5)	Purple
5	25 (inc 5)	Purple
6	30 (inc 5)	Purple
7	35 (inc 5)	Purple
8	40 (inc 5)	Purple
9	44 (inc 4)	Purple
10	48 (inc 4)	Purple
11–23	48	Purple
24	Into back loops 48	Purple
25	36 (dec 12)	Purple
26	30 (dec 6)	Purple
27	20 (dec 10)	Purple
Sew on eyes, eyebrow and mouth. Stuff firmly		
28	10 (dec 10)	Purple
29	5 (dec 5)	Purple

PETALS

Round	Stitches	Colour
1	MC 6	Orange/Yellow
2	12 (inc 6)	Orange/Yellow
3–6	12	Orange/Yellow

mother called me petal

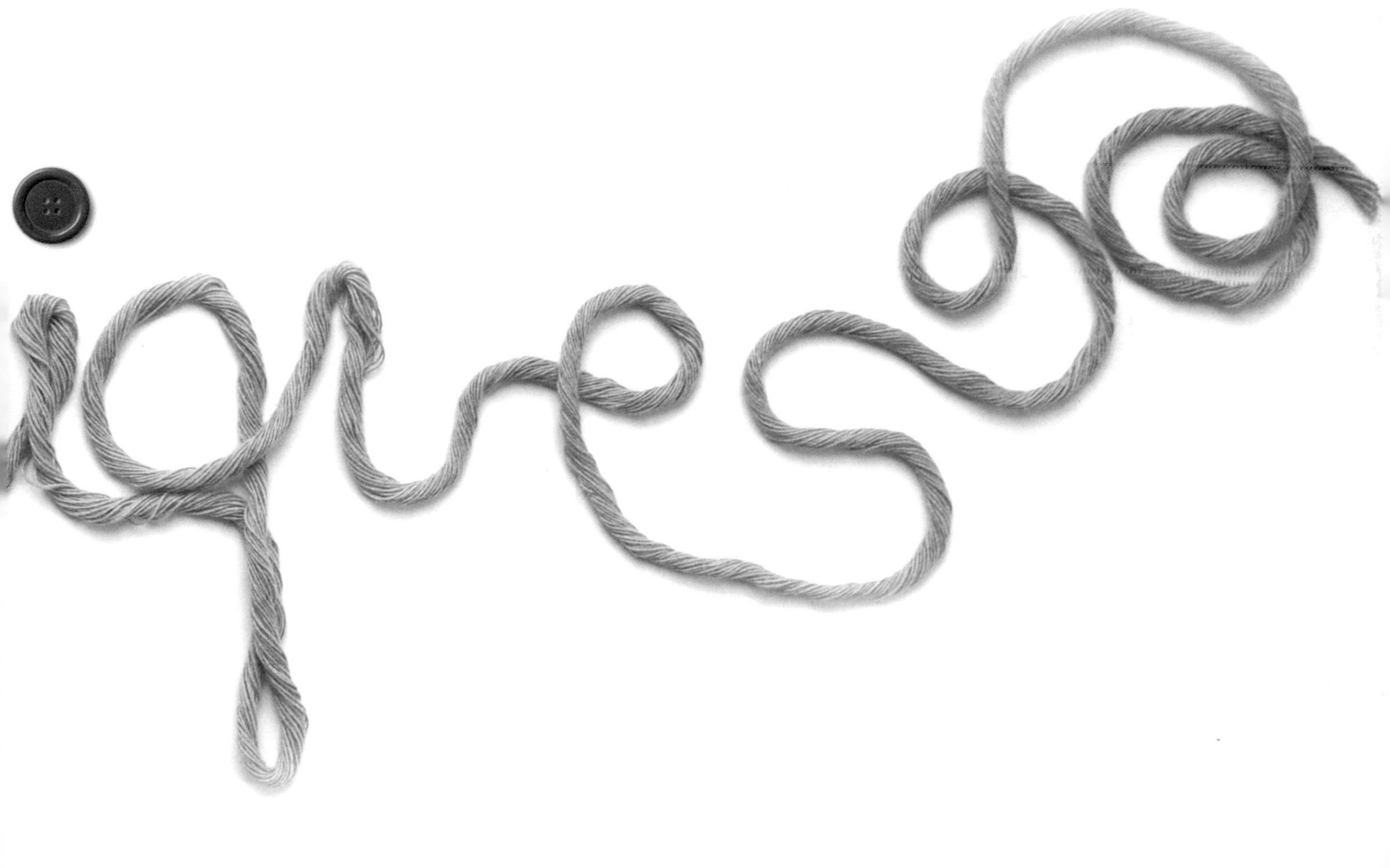

The Japanese art of amigurumi is the crocheting or knitting of cute stuffed creatures. The world derives from the Japanese words 'ami', meaning crocheted or knitted, and 'nuigurumi', which means stuffed doll.

What is amigurumi?

Amigurumi creatures, such as Bakemono, are made from yarn that is worked with a smaller size of hook than is usual for the weight of yarn. This produces a closely woven fabric without any gaps through which stuffing might escape. Amigurumi are usually worked in sections and joined, though some designs may have a head and torso but no limbs, and be worked in one piece.

The simplest amigurumi designs are worked in spirals, but unlike traditional Western crochet, which is usually made in joined rounds, the various parts are made individually, then stuffed and sewn together. A typical amigurumi toy will consist of an over-sized round head, a cylindrical body, arms and legs, plus ears and tail if appropriate. The body is usually stuffed with fibre stuffing, while limbs and other extremities are sometimes stuffed with plastic pellets to give them a lifelike weight. Safety eyes may be used, or the features may simply be embroidered on the toy.

Felt is often used to create the ears, face, or nose, and it may also be used to make cute embellishments.

Welcome to the world of amigurumi!

Crochet

once you start crocheting you'll be hooked

Crocheting is a method of creating fancy lacy patterns using yarn and a single hook. Little is known of its history, and the earliest known examples date only from the 18th century, when it first became popular in Europe. It may have evolved from traditional craft practices in Arabia, South America or China.

Originally we were knitters, and taught ourselves how to crochet from a book. We now agree that crocheting is far easier than knitting; it is simply pulling yarn through a loop. Another appealing factor is the speed of crochet, and it is convenient when travelling: no need to worry about needles poking from your bag at rush hour, or dropped stitches!

The fabric produced by crochet is different to that produced by knitting. Knitting produces regular stitches and a fabric that is usually quite stretchy. Crochet, however, produces stitches that are more compact, so the resulting fabric is denser and less stretchy. These qualities of crochet fabric mean that it is perfect for making amigurumi.

Crochet hooks

Traditional crochet hooks range from a bent needle in a cork handle to expensively crafted silver, brass, steel, ivory and bone hooks. Modern hooks are usually made from aluminium, plastic or steel, but are also available in wood and bamboo.

For amigurumi, we recommend aluminium or steel hooks. We often work with pieces that require tight, dense stitches and find metal hooks easier to use as they slip more easily between the stitches. We can also pull on them as much as we like without worrying that they will snap! The obvious disadvantage of metal hooks is that they are cold to the touch and can be very slippery, so choose what you feel comfortable with. For projects that require larger hooks or very thick yarn, it may be worth experimenting with wooden hooks because they are not as slippery as metal hooks and are available in beautiful designs.

Hooks are sized according to thickness, and the size is identified in millimetres or by a letter (US). In this book, we have used a 3.5mm hook, but any size can be used and the choice of yarn adapted accordingly. Remember that the smaller the hook, the tighter and denser the stitches. Tight, dense stitches are what you want to achieve, though not so tight that they are impossible to work! As a rough guide, hooks sized from 3–3.5mm are suitable for most cashmere-mix or acrylic Aran yarn.

Just to make things a little more interesting, there are different US and UK terms for crochet stitches. This book uses the UK name double crochet (dc) rather than the US term, single crochet (sc).

Choosing yarn

There are three main choices when considering yarn for amigurumi projects: colour, structure and weight. Beside these important choices, we also look at the practical care of your precious creations.

With children in mind, we have tried to make everything washable and easy to care for, leaving you more time to create more fun projects. We have mainly used Aran-weight yarn. The yarn chosen is durable and gives a solid finish, which helps the finished toy to hold its shape. These yarn types are twisted, so the strands are less likely to unravel, and they are also easier to work when you are using a small hook.

Colour

There are two main approaches to selecting the right colour yarn for your project: by using contrasting colours, or by using complementary colours. Contrasting colours typically work well for 'bold' projects with large pieces to make up and contrast. Complementary colours and softer shades such as pastels work well for more 'delicate' projects and smaller pieces. There are no rights or wrongs, so mix and match as you like to make your work unique, and personalized to your taste.

Colour-fastness

It is a good idea to choose a yarn that is colour-fast, especially if the finished item is intended for a child. Most modern yarn is colour-fast, but yarn produced by traditional dyeing methods may not be. For projects made in multiple shades it is particularly important to test for colour-fastness, to ensure that a dark colour will not run into a pale colour. To test, simply wet a piece of the yarn, wrap tightly round a piece of white paper towel and allow to dry. Unwind the yarn, and if the towel has changed colour the yarn is not colour-fast and may need to be dry cleaned.

Yarn structure

Yarns are made up of thin strands of spun fibre, twisted together to make up the required thickness. The twist is another important consideration: with some yarns the twist quickly unravels if you make a few mistakes and need to undo and rework. Choose a yarn with a firm twist that is less likely to unravel during the process.

Yarn weight

Yarns are generally classified into different types (see below). We have mainly used medium-weight yarn for our projects.

YARN WEIGHT

Yarn weight	Yarn type
lace	2-ply
super fine	3-ply (US fingering)
fine	4-ply (US sport); sock; baby quickerknit; lightweight DK
light	DK (US light worsted)
medium	Aran (US fisherman/worsted); Afghan
heavy	Chunky (US bulky)
very heavy	Super chunky (US extra-bulky)

Crochet techniques

Chain stitch

1 Form a slipknot on the hook. With the hook in the right hand and the yarn resting over the middle finger of the left hand, pull the yarn taut. Take the hook under, then over yarn.

2 Pull the hook and yarn through the loop, holding the slip knot steady. Repeat action to form an even chain.

Double crochet

1 Starting with a foundation chain, insert the hook into the next stitch. Wrap the yarn round the hook and draw it back through the stitch; there should now be two loops on the hook.

2 Wrap the yarn round the hook again, then draw it through both loops so there is one loop left on the hook. Repeat across the row.

never be afraid to express yourself

Sewing and finishing techniques

Hiding yarn tails

Thread or stitch the tail into a section of the body that is the same colour and then pull out on the other side of the body piece (it's best to squeeze the body piece if the needle is too short). Trim so that the yarn is in line with the body and therefore hidden.

Making hair

Using a needle, thread 2in (5cm) strands of yarn through the stitches on the head or body and knot using an overhand knot. You can use a double overhand knot if you wish, to make it extra secure.

Closing a hole

Finish off a hole by crocheting two stitches into one until the hole tightens and closes.

Blanket stitch

Work from left to right. Bring needle up at point A, down at B and up at C with thread looped under the needle. Pull through. Take care to tighten the stitches equally. Repeat to the right. Fasten the last loop by taking a small stitch along the lower line. When the stitch is used to join or edge, the bottom of the 'U' shape should lie on the outer edge of the fabric to form a raised line.

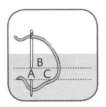 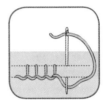

Sewing up

This is an important stage, as you do not want all your hard work to be ruined by the toy falling apart. Most of the stuffing and sewing up necessary for your amigurumi will be done as you go along, so there will be no need for major assembly at the end.

Sewing up is usually done using the yarn ends left when the initial magic circle is made. Using a darning needle, take small, neat stitches and try to make them show as little as possible. Fasten off yarn ends securely by taking several stitches through your work.

i'm ready for my close-up

Josephine (left) and Lan-Anh at the launch of their previous book, *Amigurumi*, in London in 2010.

Fun with Bakemono

i am made from inspiration

After the success of their book, *Amigurumi*, which formed part of the Cozy series, Lan-Anh and Josephine were not able to resist the invitation to create another book on crocheted toys.

Creating cute crocheted creatures is a passion the best friends share, and this time the theme they thought of was monsters. This led to a creative sketched storyboard of all the beasts and the eventual making of the Bakemono gang.

Lan-Anh and Josephine hope that what they have created is a book of inspirations rather than just a book of patterns and instructions. They hope that, using the basic framework for each creature, you will be able to personalize and create your own Bakemono to keep or as a gift for someone you care about.

Lan-Anh and Josephine hope you enjoy your Bakemono adventure.

Lan-Anh: Thank you to my husband **Vi** for the **inspirations** – without you the book would **still be** half-formed sketches **on the coffee table**. You kept me **motivated** and the threats (from you) and **tantrums** (from me) have paid off. Finally, thank you to **my family** for everything.

Josephine: Thank you to both **Lewis** and **Sam** for being my inspiration and my parents, **Margaret** and **Michael**, for their endless support in all that I do. Special thanks to my siblings **Tiffany**, **Cassie** and **Gebbies** who have always been there for me, and have **never doubted my dreams** and ideas, no matter how crazy they might be.

index

To place an order, or to request a catalogue, contact:
GMC Publications Ltd, Castle Place, 166 High Street, Lewes,
East Sussex, BN7 1XU, United Kingdom
Tel: +44 (0)1273 488005 Fax: +44 (0)1273 402866 www.gmcbooks.com